PIZZA PLUS

This is the complete book on pizza – and more! From the traditional Neapolitan pizza to the more fanciful creations of some of today's most innovative Italian chefs, Vincenzo Buonassisi shows how pizza is taking on a whole new look and taste.

Starting with a single recipe for classic pizza dough, the book presents an exciting choice of delicious toppings and shows how to experiment with your own ideas. Recipes range from the humble pizza margherita, to the exotic such as pizza macedonia, made with courgettes, green pepper and plums.

Pizza is basically a thin layer of dough baked with a topping of one's choice. Vincenzo Buonassisi takes a wider view. He gives recipes from around the world which use a similar dough base – from the Italian calzone, focaccia and torta rustica, to the Indian chapati, Middle Eastern pitta, Mexican tortilla and blinis from Russia – and reveals the pizza in all its variations.

Pizza Plus makes them easy to cook, nutritious, and fun to eat – for all occasions.

VINCENZO BUONASSISI – described in the *New York Times* as 'the Italian food authority' – is a prolific author of books on Italian cookery, on gastronomy and the history of food. Born during World War I in central Italy, in Aquila, his formative years were spent in southern Italy, in Cerignolo. Later his family moved to Rome, where Vincenzo Buonassisi continued his studies, finally graduating in law. Called up to serve in World War II, he was captured in Tunisia and spent two years in America as a prisoner of war. On his return to Italy, he worked and travelled widely until 1973 as a journalist specializing in the arts for the prestigious Milan newspaper *Corriere della Sera*. Since then he has worked for Italian television, contributed to leading Italian magazines and is a consultant for *Vini e Liquori* (Wines and Liqueurs).

SCOTT EWING, who adapted and edited this edition of Vincenzo Buonassisi's book, is a cookery journalist, food consultant and enthusiast who graduated from the University of Texas and Oxford University. Living in England since 1975, he has written for magazines, edited a number of cookery books and for three years was international cookery editor of the best-selling cookery partwork magazine, *Robert Carrier's Kitchen*.

This book is dedicated to Andrea and
all other lovers of real pizza

VINCENZO BUONASSISI

COLLINS

First published in 1984 by
William Collins Sons & Co Ltd

© 1982 Gruppo Editoriale Fabbri S.p.A., Milan

Adapted and edited by Scott Ewing

Photographs by Angelo Cattaneo and Ivo Morellini
Cover photograph by Pierro Baguzzi

Printed in Italy
Typesetting by Chambers Wallace, London

ISB 0 00 411202 4

Contents

Introduction

It was not until the eighteenth century that the pizza of pizzas – pizza made with tomatoes – first appeared. The reason for its tardy appearance is the same as that for spaghetti with tomato sauce, another dish that conquered Naples and went on to conquer the world. Tomatoes simply were not introduced to Europe from the 'New World' of the Americas until the sixteenth century. Then it took a century and a half for Europeans to discover their culinary value and for Neapolitans in particular to incorporate them into their cooking.

Tomato pizza is therefore a relatively recent arrival in the history of food. Yet it is this pizza which has gained worldwide popularity and is generally the image that people have when they think of pizza. That there are pizzarias all over the world today attests to its success.

Today's pizza is a piece of leavened dough, usually baked as a round with a wide variety of toppings.

Versions of pizza have been known in southern Italy since ancient times, some topped with olives and pork scraps, others with honey, raisins and pine nuts. Made with unleavened dough, they were eaten by both the Greeks and Romans and, thanks to the poet Virgil, we have the recipe for one, *moretum*. It was a flat circle of unleavened dough, baked and – like today's *schiacciata* – eaten as bread, sometimes with oil and herbs, sometimes with raw onions or garlic.

Though this early unleavened *schiacciata* was a part of Italian life from Roman times to the medieval period and beyond, historical records refer to it again around the year 1000 A.D. – a time when many people were expecting the end of the world, but when the Neapolitans were thinking of food! In that period in Naples, instead of *schiacciata*, people spoke of *lagano*, a word coming from the Latin *laganum* and the Greek *laganon*. The unleavened dough was roasted and cut into strips which were then tossed into a pot of vegetables or other ingredients cooking over the fire. *Laganon* was, in short, a kind of primitive *tagliatelle*, or noodle. (On the islands of Sicily and Sardinia, in fact, tagliatelle is still called *laganella*.) Horace, another Roman poet, wrote gluttonously of a soup of chick peas, leeks and *lagano* made in southern Italy. The dish is still made there, but now the strips of dough are fried before adding them to the soup.

Although people in Naples spoke of *lagano* around the year 1000 A.D., the word *picea* began to appear also. It might have been another name for *lagano* or it might have indicated a new dish, a circle of dough covered with various ingredients before baking. Shortly afterwards, the word *piza* came into usage. Yet it was sometime later – when dough was leavened, topped with simple ingredients and baked – that we have the beginning of actual *pizza* and its near relation, today's round, pitta-like bread, *schiacciata*.

Towards the end of the eighteenth century in Naples, pizza emerged as a distinctive dish. The first pizzas were probably flavoured with oil and garlic, with Mozzarella cheese and salted anchovies or covered with tiny fish called *cincinielli*. Historical records also speak of a pizza folded over like a book – probably an early form of *calzone*, pizza dough folded into a halfmoon shape around a stuffing and baked.

Up to 1830, pizza was sold from open-air stands in Naples. In that year the existence of a true pizzeria is recorded. Called Port'Alba and located in Naples, it had a wood-fired oven lined with bricks. That was soon replaced with an oven lined inside with volcanic rock from Mount Vesuvius which was able to reach the higher temperatures needed to make the best pizzas. Port'Alba became the haunt of artists and writers. Certainly among the most celebrated guests of the time was Salvatore di Giacomo who dedicated several poems to pizza.

Many other poets, writers and musicians have been inspired by pizza. Alexander Dumas, the author of *The Three Musketeers*, was one. In a series of travel essays he makes some sharp observations and gives odd information about pizza. He writes, for example, that 'the pizza is a kind of "stiacciata" which is made in St. Denis: it is round in shape and made with bread dough. At first glance it looks like simple food, but when examined more closely it seems complicated.' He was right. His reference to the schiacciata of St. Denis suggests that variations on the pizza theme were widespread. Yet the garnishing and cooking of pizza were perfected in Naples.

Dumas also notes various kinds of pizza, the most common ones at the beginning of the nineteenth century being those garnished with oil, lard, pork fat, cheese, tomatoes and small fish. In passing, he mentions a pizza called 'a otto' which he says was baked a week before it was eaten. Here he made an error. The pizza 'for eight' was eaten right away, but it was paid for eight days later, even though these easy terms increased its cost a little. This custom lasted for years and perhaps still exists in Naples today.

Pizza is often mentioned in a famous opera, *Usi e costumi di Napoli*, by a composer with a French name, De Broucard, but who was completely Neapolitanized. His text, written around 1850, says that the word 'pizza' did not even exist in the 'vocabolario della Crusca', the dialect of a Florentine group which tried to maintain the purity of the Italian language. The reason, he maintained, was that pizza is made with flour, an ingredient the group considered vulgar. They also refused to recognize pizza because it was a speciality of Naples, a rival city.

De Broucard's text says, 'Take a piece of dough, pull it or spread it with a rolling pin or push it out with the palm of your hand, put whatever comes into your head on it, season it with oil or lard, eat it and you will know what pizza is.' In the opera he lists the most common pizzas. There are oil and garlic pizzas, pizzas with grated cheese, lard, basil or tiny fish, with Mozzarella, with ham or mussels, and the tomato pizza, though this last one he did not consider of great importance.

In the summer of 1889, King Umberto I and Queen Margherita of Italy went to the Campodimonti Palace in Naples, from where the king was to sail to the islands of Sicily and Sardinia. The queen was curious about pizza. She had never eaten it but had heard much about it from writers and artists who had visited the court in Rome. Since the queen could not visit a pizzeria, the pizzeria had to come to her. Thus it was that the most famous pizza maker of the time, don Raffaele Esposito, the owner of a celebrated pizzeria, Pietro il Pizzaiuolo, was called to the palace.

Assisted by his wife donna Rosa, the true mistress of pizza, don Raffaele used the royal ovens to prepare one pizza with pork fat, cheese and basil, one with garlic, oil and tomatoes, and another made with tomatoes, Mozzarella and fresh basil, the colours – red, white and green – of the Italian flag. The last one particularly pleased Queen Margherita and not just for patriotic reasons! A good public relations man, don Raffaele seized his chance and named the pizza 'alla Margherita' and the next day added it to the menu at his pizzeria. Soon the red, white and green pizza became famous in Naples.

As the story was told outside of Naples, this pizza's popularity spread and eventually it was called simply 'pizza margherita'. Curiously, what passed as don Raffaele's 'creation' had already existed. Although the tomato, Mozzarella and basil pizza was not considered among the classic or most important pizzas, it was already being made in Naples. The earlier, Bourbon queen, Maria Carolina, was such a glutton for pizza that she wanted a pizza oven built in her palace. She also loved the same tri-coloured pizza. She might not have been so enthusiastic, however, if she had known that those colours would represent another dynasty which would overthrow hers and unite the kingdoms of Italy.

The popularity of pizza margherita helped spread pizza's fame, first to northern Italy and then to the world. The two pizzas which have travelled the farthest are the margherita and the neapolitan (made like the margherita, but with anchovies added).

There are a wealth of recipes in this book, because I wanted to give a true picture of pizza. Pizza has developed over many centuries from its beginnings as a flat bread topped with salt, pork scraps or other simple ingredients into several different shapes and dough bases with an enormous variety of delicious fillings. I have given the more traditional pizzas as well as others that might be called fantasy variations. These are the personal creations of pizza makers who were inspired by the regions of Italy they came from or by the places they worked. I could have included many more recipes of this sort, but I chose those which had a special character and left out others whose ingredients were too vague or extreme.

Then I added recipes from others parts of Italy and the world that are related to pizza because of their dough base. For instance, I have included savoury rustic tarts, *torte rustiche*, made with the original pizza's simple flour and water dough but enriched with oil, lard or even eggs and other ingredients. There are also recipes for varieties of pizza which are sometimes stuffed and baked or fried.

As all the recipes can be made easily at home, I hope this book will give you a wider repertoire of truly enjoyable dishes to share with your friends and family.

How to make a pizza base

The classic recipe uses flour, yeast, salt and water, but the dough requires particular care and attention to get the best result. My recipe for it will make six small to medium-sized pizzas, depending on how thinly you roll out the dough. You will need:

800 g / 1¾ lb preferably strong white flour, though plain flour could be used instead

40 g / 1½ oz fresh yeast, or 20 g / ¾ oz dried active baking yeast

125 ml / 4 fl oz lukewarm water

5 ml / 1 tsp salt

Crumble or stir the yeast into the lukewarm water and let it sit for 10 minutes. Meanwhile, sift about 175 g / 6 oz of the flour onto a pastry board and make a well in the centre. Pour in the dissolved yeast and work in the flour until you have a rather *fig 1* sticky ball. Put the ball into a lightly floured bowl and make a cross on top with the *fig 2* tip of a knife. Cover the bowl with a cloth and let it rest in a warm, draught-free *fig 3* place for 1 hour.

This part of the recipe can be shortened to 30 minutes by placing the dough in a slightly warmer spot and slightly increasing the amount of yeast. Experts agree, however, that the first method is best.

Now you have a leavened dough. Sift the rest of the flour on your pastry board, *fig 4* sprinkle over the salt and put the leavened dough in the middle. Begin to knead the dough, salt and flour together, mixing well, using the heel of your hand to push forward and pull back. Gradually add about 350 ml / 12 fl oz warm water if necessary, so that the dough doesn't become too dry and crumble. It should take about 10 minutes until the dough becomes smooth and rather elastic. The kneading eliminates the excess gas produced by the yeast and works the ingredients together.

Now, divide the dough into six portions, place them on a lightly floured surface in *fig 5* a warm, draught-free place, cover with a cloth and let them rise again until doubled in size. This usually takes 1–2 hours, but judge this by your eye.

Punch the risen dough down and knead each portion until it can be rolled into *fig 6* a circle. Accomplished pizza makers enjoy doing acrobatics with the dough at this stage, throwing the circle of dough into the air and catching it without it folding or losing its shape just to show how elastic the dough is. (If you are unable to use the dough immediately, you can store the kneaded portions in an airtight container and refrigerate for several days or freeze them for up to 2 months. Allow them to come to room temperature before rolling them out.)

The recipe for the dough base given here will not be repeated for the many pizzas in the following section. There is enough dough in the recipe for six medium-sized

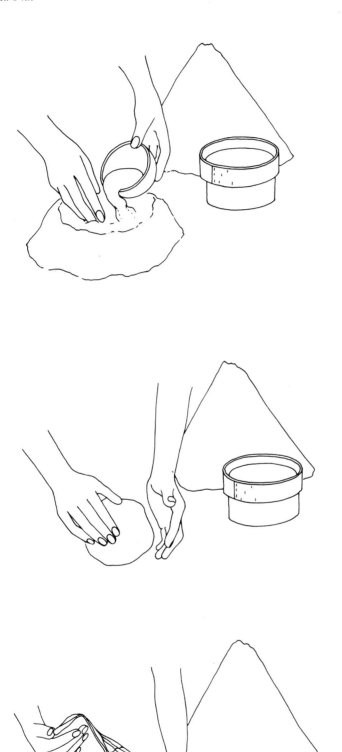

fig 1

fig 2

fig 3

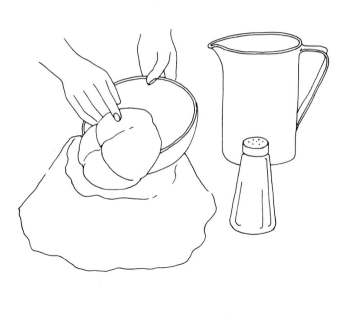

fig 4

fig 5

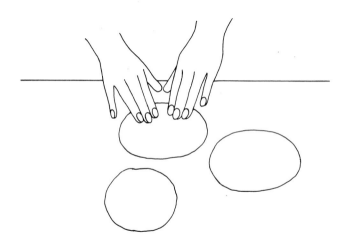

fig 6

pizza bases, each about 20–23 cm/8–9 in diameter and enough for 1 person. You can adjust the quantities for the dough and filling ingredients proportionally to make more or fewer pizzas. If you plan to make many pizzas, it is better to make the dough in two or more batches, then chill or freeze the unused portions. You can cook them on a baking sheet or tray – no special 'pizza tin' is necessary. An average-sized oven will easily cook two of these pizzas at a time. It may be necessary to cook three or more pizzas in succession.

How big and how thick should the circle of dough be? In general the dough should be thin, but there are two schools of thought, the classic Neapolitan and the Roman. Neapolitan pizza should be a little over 3 mm/$\frac{1}{8}$ in thick, with the centre a little thinner and the edges a little thicker. The edges will puff up a little during baking, forming a rim which serves to keep the ingredients in the centre. The Roman school of thought says that the dough should be a little thinner, no more than 3 mm/$\frac{1}{8}$ in thick, with no rim as Roman fillings are less fluid and so tend to stay in place. In reality, how you roll your dough depends more on what you are going to put on top.

Now the dough is ready to be topped with the ingredients from one of the recipes in the next section and baked. The baking time should be short and intense, so the oven should be preheated to 220 C/425 F/gas 7. Ideally pizza is baked in a brick oven or one lined with volcanic rock and fueled with wood, but a gas or electric oven will do nicely if the dough is baked on the middle or upper (ie, hotter) shelves.

In traditional pizza-making, the pizza is baked on a large flat wooden spatula with a long wooden handle. The pizza maker watches the pizza through the oven window and knows exactly when to remove it so that it slides, perfectly cooked, onto the serving plate. But when is the exact moment? If the pizza has a rim, it is easy to tell as the dough becomes golden brown and small blisters develop on its surface. If the pizza has no rim, look at its edges; they should also be baked to a golden brown. It is not as easy to check in ovens without windows, but when the Mozzarella or other cheeses look melted or when the other ingredients become shiny because of the oil they were moistened with, the pizza is ready, usually 10–15 minutes.

And the shape? Besides the traditional round pizza, in Italy pizza is also made in a rectangle. This became famous a few decades ago in the Sorrento peninsula, but the only difference is the shape. The pizza is baked on a rectangular pan with or without a rim and is then cut across into slices as long and wide as you wish.

The following recipes for pizza toppings will fill either one or six of the individual-sized pizza bases as indicated in each recipe. The amounts given in each recipe are only a guide. You can vary the amounts and the ingredients. Of course, it is better not to increase the topping ingredients too much so they do not cook well or make them so scant that the topping cooks too fast and burns (not to mention that the pizza will also end up being dull).

Remember that olive oil has a lovely, distinctive flavour and it is used fairly liberally in Italy. When a recipe calls for olive oil to dribble over pizza before baking it, plan to use at least 15 ml/1 tbls oil per 20–23 cm/8–9 in diameter pizza unless the recipe indicates otherwise.

Basic topping ingredients such as Mozarella or other cheeses and tomatoes should always be in large enough quantities to cover the dough base completely, leaving only a small border. They should rarely be thicker than the dough itself. Do not overwhelm the pizza with garnishes such as sausage or bacon slices or anchovies. There should be just enough to add flavour. Canned, drained tomatoes can be substituted for fresh tomatoes. In short, there are few hard and fast rules regarding pizza toppings; with a little care you can't go wrong.

The recipes in this book are given in metric and imperial measures. Follow *either* the metric *or* the imperial measures as they are not interchangeable. Australians should remember that their tablespoon differs from the British tablespoon. The tablespoon used throughout the book has been the British metric tablespoon which holds 15 millilitres, but the Australian metric tablespoon holds 20 millilitres. A teaspoon holds about 5 millilitres in both countries.

For recipes in the rest of the book which are based on variations of the pizza base, I have tried to indicate the amounts and procedures for preparation in each case. While these variations may be minimal, I know from experience that it is annoying to constantly have to refer back to previous pages to make a dish. The only exception to this is when a series of similar recipes are grouped together, such as the varieties of *torte rusticche* (country quiches), where only the fillings change.

Finally, how do you eat pizza? Let us be very clear about this. Pizza should always be eaten with your hands, just as they do in Naples. It doesn't make sense to subject a pizza to the torture of a knife and fork while it cools, losing its flavour and aroma. Pizza originally was not very large or heavily sauced and it was easy to fold it in half to eat, taking care not to drip the oil, Mozzarella and tomato. However, today's pizzas are bigger and richer and therein lies the problem. The simplest solution is to cut the pizza into four or six pieces, fold them and hold them with your hands to eat. Then the delightful flavour and aroma are not lost. So enjoy making and eating your pizzas – *buon appetito!*

TOMATO SAUCE FOR PIZZA

1 kg / 2¼ lb firm ripe tomatoes
30 ml / 2 fl oz olive oil
5 ml / 1 tsp sugar
salt (optional)

Halve the tomatoes and squeeze out the seeds and all the liquid or remove them with a spoon. Put the tomato halves in a saucepan with the oil and sugar and cook over low heat for about 7 minutes, stirring frequently. Put the tomato mixture in a sieve and let it drain over a bowl for about 10 minutes, then discard the watery liquid. Replace the bowl and press the tomato mixture through the sieve or put it through a vegetable mill to remove the skins. Add salt, if wished. If not needed immediately, allow the sauce to cool, then refrigerate up to 5 days. Makes about 250 ml / 9 fl oz sauce.

PART ONE

Pizza, schiacciate and calzoni

A huge selection of pizza toppings are found here, from the deliciously simple to the sinfully elaborate. There is also a selection of recipes of the bread-like *schiacciate* and the stuffed, half-moon-shaped *calzone* – a pizza you can take a walk with!

1 PIZZA WITH OIL AND GARLIC

The custom of eating slices of bread flavoured with oil and garlic as an accompaniment to pasta is surely a very old one. These flavours were first used to enrich the taste of the *schiacciata*, a kind of pitta bread traditionally eaten in Italy. The custom was continued with pizza.

Basic dough recipe, page **15**   *Fills 6 pizzas*
6–12 garlic cloves, thinly sliced
90 ml / 6 tbls olive oil   Salt and freshly ground black pepper

Heat the oven to 220 C / 425 F / gas 7. Roll out the dough into circles and bake on a large baking sheet until golden brown. Remove them from the oven and moisten the tops with olive oil, sprinkle with the garlic slices, salt and pepper and serve hot.

2 BAKED PIZZA WITH OIL AND GARLIC

This recipe varies from the previous one in that you moisten the unbaked dough with a little more olive oil, sprinkle over sliced garlic and salt and then bake. A pinch of oregano or rosemary can be added for flavour. Pepper should only be added after the pizza is baked.

3 PIZZA WITH LARD AND CHEESE

Basic dough recipe   *Fills 6 pizzas*
75 g / 3 oz lard, softened
225 g / 8 oz Provolone, Pecorino or Caciocavallo cheese, grated
Fresh basil leaves

Baked pizza with oil and garlic

Heat the oven to 220C/425F/gas 7 and roll out the dough. Brush the dough lightly with the lard, sprinkle with the grated cheese and garnish with a few leaves of fresh basil. Remember that fresh basil leaves should never be washed or they lose their fragrance. Simply wipe each leaf with a soft cloth. Bake until golden.

4 PIZZA NEAPOLITAN

This is considered the most traditional pizza today: it evolved from the original oil and garlic pizza.

Basic dough recipe   *Fills 6 pizzas*

18 medium-sized tomatoes, blanched, peeled, halved, seeded and flattened

Fresh basil leaves, wiped clean, or oregano

About 6 garlic cloves, finely sliced   Olive oil   Salt

Heat the oven to 220C/425F/gas 7 and roll out the dough. On each circle of dough place 6 flattened halves of tomato. Sprinkle over some basil leaves or oregano or both. Add the finely sliced garlic to taste, then dribble olive oil over the whole pizza, add salt and bake.

Note: the filling should not go right to the edge of the dough. Instead leave a margin of 12 mm/$\frac{1}{2}$ in around it. The uncovered dough will expand and puff up during baking forming a low crust around the edge.

The tomatoes can be chopped or sliced, but in every case the seeds and the watery interior should be removed beforehand or the dough will become soggy and not cook properly.

Pizza neapolitan

5 PIZZA ALLA MARINARA

This is another variation of the most traditional pizzas. It is made more or less as the Neapolitan pizza, except that it omits oregano and basil.

    Basic dough recipe   *Fills 6 pizzas*
    18 medium-sized tomatoes, blanched, peeled, halved, seeded and flattened
    6 garlic cloves, finely sliced
    1–2 anchovy fillets per pizza, washed and chopped
    Olive oil   Black olives, stoned and sliced (optional)

Heat the oven to 220 C/425 F/gas 7 and roll out the dough. Place the tomatoes and garlic slices on the dough, then scatter the chopped anchovies over the surface. Finally dribble olive oil over the entire filling and bake until golden.

If you are very fond of anchovies, you might want to position whole, washed anchovy fillets on top of the pizza like the spokes of a wheel with one in the middle wrapped round a piece of garlic.

Another common variation is to also scatter slices of black olives over the pizza as their flavour goes very well with the other ingredients.

Pizza alla marinara

6 PIZZA MARGHERITA

Pizza margherita takes its name from Queen Margherita of Savoy. It was first served to her one evening in 1889 at a party in the Capodimonte Palace in Naples. The queen loved it for its flavour and for its red, white and green colours – the colours of the Italian flag. Actually, this tri-coloured pizza was already known when Queen Margherita first tasted it. Carolina, an earlier Bourbon queen was also very fond of it.

    Basic pizza dough   *Fills 6 pizzas*
    12–18 medium-sized tomatoes, blanched, peeled, halved and seeded, then
        chopped   500 g/18 oz Mozzarella cheese, cut into thin slices
    Fresh basil leaves, wiped clean   Salt   Olive oil

Heat the oven to 220 C/425 F/gas 7 and roll out the dough. Spread the tomatoes over the dough, then the Mozzarella. Scatter basil leaves over the top, salt to taste and moisten with a little olive oil. Bake until golden.

Pizza margherita

7   PIZZA ROMAN-STYLE

Basic pizza dough   *Fills 6 pizzas*
18 medium-sized tomatoes, blanched, peeled, halved, seeded and flattened
    or 800 g / 1½ lb canned tomatoes, drained and chopped
500 g / 18 oz Mozzarella cheese, sliced   Anchovy fillets to taste
Fresh basil leaves, wiped clean   Olive oil

Heat the oven to 220 C / 425 F / gas 7. Roll out the dough very thinly so that it becomes crisp as it bakes. Spread the tomatoes on the dough, then the Mozzarella slices, the anchovies, and a few basil leaves and dribble oil over the whole circle. Bake until golden and crisp.

8 PIZZA WITH ONIONS [1]

Basic dough recipe   *Fills 6 pizzas*
6 medium-sized onions, thinly sliced
175 g/6 oz Pecorino or Romano cheese, grated   Olive oil
Freshly ground black pepper (optional)

Heat the oven to 220 C/425 F/gas 7 and roll out the dough. Spread a layer of onions on the dough and sprinkle over enough grated cheese to cover. Moisten the whole pizza with oil and bake until golden. It will look like a brightly shining sun on the plate. Many add a sprinkling of freshly ground pepper after it is baked.

In other versions, strong cheeses like Provolone or Caciocavallo, grated, can be used. Some also use grated Parmesan instead, but it is less effective as the pizza is then too delicate in flavour.

9 PIZZA WITH ONIONS [2]

Pizza with onions [1]

This recipe is identical to **8** except that you spread a little canned, drained and chopped tomato on the dough first, then the onions and cheese are spread over the dough and oil is dribbled over all. The pizza comes out with a delicate and pleasing rosy colour.

10 PIZZA WITH ONIONS [3]

Basic dough recipe   *Fills 6 pizzas*
6 medium-sized onions   Olive oil
9 medium-sized tomatoes, blanched, peeled, halved, seeded and chopped
Salt and freshly ground black pepper
500 g/18 oz Mozzarella, cubed   6–12 anchovy fillets, washed and chopped
175 g/6 oz Pecorino or Romano cheese, grated

Heat the oven to 220 C/425 F/gas 7 and roll out the dough. Slice the onions and sauté them in a little oil until translucent. Do not let them brown. Add the tomatoes, season with salt and pepper and stir briefly. Spread this sauce over the dough, sprinkle over the Mozzarella and anchovies, then the grated Pecorino or Romano. Bake until golden and cheese is melted.

In Sardinia where this recipe is popular, oregano is often mixed in with the grated cheese before it is sprinkled over the pizza.

11 PIZZA PUGLIESE-STYLE

My friends make this at the Porta Rossa restaurant in Milan. They and the recipe are from the south, from Apricena in Gargano, a place where the Emperor Frederick II loved to go wild boar hunting.

Basic dough recipe   *Fills 6 pizzas*
4–6 garlic cloves, finely sliced   Fresh basil leaves, wiped clean
25 g/1 oz chopped parsley
900 g/2 lb tomatoes, blanched, peeled, halved, seeded and chopped
175 g/6 oz Pecorino or Romano cheese, grated   Oregano
Freshly ground black pepper

Heat the oven to 220 C/425 F/gas 7 and roll out the dough. Chop the garlic, basil and parsley together, mixing well. Spread the chopped tomato over the circles of dough, then spread over the garlic, basil and parsley mixture. Sprinkle the grated cheese and a pinch of oregano over each one and bake until golden and the cheese has melted. At the table, grind some black pepper on top.

12 PIZZA WITH GREENS [1]

Basic dough recipe   *Fills 6 pizzas*
900 g / 2 lb fresh spinach or beet spinach, trimmed
175 g / 6 oz Parmesan, Pecorino or Provolone cheese, grated
Olive oil   Salt

Heat the oven to 220 C / 425 F / gas 7. Wash and drain the greens well, then chop them finely. Roll out the dough, making six circles. They should not be too thin. Spread the spinach or spring greens over each one. Generously sprinkle the cheese over them, mashing it into the greens a little. Moisten each circle with a little oil, sprinkle with salt and bake until golden. Eat the pizza while it is hot and crispy.

13 PIZZA WITH GREENS [2]

In this version you can chop beet spinach, spinach, batavia or other greens together finely. Make a layer of chopped greens on the dough, then the grated cheese. If using beet spinach, lay a few large leaves on top and garnish with Mozzarella cheese. Moisten with olive oil, season with salt and bake.

14 PIZZA WITH PEPPERS [1]

Basic dough recipe   *Fills 6 pizzas*
6 medium-sized green peppers
500 g / 18 oz tomatoes, blanched, peeled, halved, seeded and chopped
Salt and coarsely ground black pepper

Heat the oven to 220 C / 425 F / gas 7. Roast the peppers first, turning them either directly over a flame or under the grill. Peel off the blackened skin, then cut them into thin strips. Roll out thin circles of dough and spread the chopped tomatoes over

Pizza with pepper [1]

Pizza with greens [2]

them. Lay the pepper strips on top and season with salt. Bake until the crust is golden and the peppers are soft. Sprinkle with coarsely ground pepper and serve while still crisp and hot.

15   PIZZA WITH PEPPERS [2]

In this version, spread about 175g/6oz grated hard cheese over the peppers. Pecorino is the preferred cheese, but Parmesan, Gruyère or Caciocavallo also work well.

16   PIZZA WITH ONIONS AND PEPPER [1]

Basic dough recipe   *Fills 6 pizzas*
225g/8oz chopped onions
3 medium-sized peppers, prepared as in recipe **14**   Olive oil

Heat the oven to 220C/425F/gas 7 and prepare the peppers. Roll out thin circles of dough. Spread a mixture of chopped onions and green pepper strips over the

Pizza with onions and peppers [2]

dough. Sprinkle with oil and bake until the peppers have become soft and the onion is cooked. The proportions of peppers to onions can be modified, using more onion and less pepper, or you can use both red and green peppers to give the pizza colour.

17   PIZZA WITH ONIONS AND PEPPERS [2]

In this version gently sauté the chopped onions in a little olive oil until translucent but not browned. Add the pepper, either chopped or in strips and let them cook gently with the onion a few minutes. Drain the onions and peppers well to get rid of as much of the cooking oil as possible, then spread them over the dough. Dribble a little fresh oil over, add a very little salt and bake until the dough is golden brown.

18   PIZZA WITH COURGETTES [1]

Basic dough recipe   *Fills 6 pizzas*
6 medium-sized courgettes   Olive oil   · Salt   25 g / 1 oz parsley
500 g / 18 oz Mozzarella, sliced

Pizza with courgettes [1]

Pizza with cardoons

Heat the oven to 220 C / 425 F / gas 7 and roll out the dough. Wash the courgettes, cut them into slices or cubes and sauté them with a little oil, salt and the parsley. Remove from the heat and drain well. Spread the mixture over the dough and add the Mozzarella slices. Dribble some more oil over the circles of dough, add a little salt and bake until golden. Serve hot.

19   PIZZA WITH COURGETTES [2]

This is the same recipe as described above with the variation of adding tomatoes, giving it a reddish colour. When you sauté the courgettes, add 3 tablespoons of drained, chopped, canned tomatoes or better yet, blanched, peeled, halved and seeded tomatoes, cut into chunks. Let the courgettes and tomato sauté a few minutes, then pour this over the pizza dough as in the preceding recipe, moisten with a little more oil and bake until golden. Serve immediately.

In this second version you can also add green or black olives, to taste, stoned and chopped.

20   PIZZA WITH FENNEL

Basic dough recipe   *Fills 6 pizzas*
1 medium-sized onion, finely chopped   Olive oil
3 large or 4 medium-sized bulbs of fennel, thinly sliced

Pizza with asparagus tips

Salt and freshly ground black pepper
175 g / 6 oz Parmesan or Pecorino cheese, grated

Heat the oven to 220 C / 425 F / gas 7 and roll out the dough. Gently sauté the onion in a little oil until translucent but not browned, then add the sliced fennel, stirring occasionally, and let it brown a little so that it loses its raw quality. Add salt and pepper and spread this mixture over the pizza dough. Sprinkle each round with grated cheese, moisten with a little oil and bake until golden.

21   PIZZA WITH CARDOONS

Cardoons are a kind of white thistle, called *cardi* in Italy. They can be replaced with peeled burdock stems. You will need about 50 g / 2 oz per serving. Simmer them briefly, then drain well. Follow the recipe for Pizza with Fennel **20**, decorating, if wished, with canned, drained, puréed tomatoes before baking.

22   PIZZA WITH ASPARAGUS TIPS

Basic dough recipe   *Fills 6 pizzas*
4 anchovy fillets, washed   Olive oil
1.4 kg / 3 lb thin asparagus stalks, tough bottoms removed
175 g / 6 oz Parmesan or Pecorino cheese, grated

Heat the oven to 220 C / 425 F / gas 7 and roll out the dough. Mash the anchovies and mix in a little oil, making a sauce. Spread this over the pizza dough. Simmer the asparagus stalks until half-cooked, about 5 minutes, then drain well, trim and arrange them over the dough. Sprinkle over the grated cheese and bake until the cheese melts and the asparagus is cooked.

You can also add canned, drained, chopped tomatoes or blanched, peeled, halved and seeded tomatoes, either flattened or chopped.

23   PIZZA WITH OLIVES

Olives are present in many kinds of pizza as a garnish, but in this pizza they play the main role.

Basic dough recipe   *Fills 6 pizzas*
900 g / 2 lb tomatoes, blanched, peeled, halved, seeded and chopped
500 g / 18 oz Mozzarella cheese, cubed
275 g / 10 oz olives, stoned and chopped

Heat the oven to 220 C / 425 F / gas 7 and roll out the dough. Spread the tomatoes over the dough, then the Mozzarella and the green olives, dribble oil over each pizza and bake until the cheese has melted and the crust is browned.

In other versions you can add chopped anchovies, about 1 fillet per pizza, and some capers and eliminate the tomatoes, if wished. Black olives can be used instead of green, but they have a stronger flavour, so fewer should be used.

24   PIZZA WITH OLIVE CAVIAR

This pizza is given its name mostly in jest. It is made with a preparation of crushed olives marinated in herbs and oil, usually marjoram, thyme or whatever is on hand. It originates from Liguria but can be found in gourmet stores carrying Italian products. You will need 15–30 ml / 1–2 tbls and 500 g / 18 oz of Mozzarella cheese per pizza. Mix the olive caviar, which is strongly flavoured, with cubes of cheese. Cover the pizza dough with this mixture and moisten with a little olive oil. Bake in a 220 C / 425 F / gas 7 oven until the crust is golden and the cheese is melted.

25   PIZZA WITH SHALLOTS

Shallots are a kind of wild onion that have a slightly bitter taste.
Basic dough recipe   *Fills 1 pizza*
12 large red or white shallots   40 g / 1½ oz Pecorino or Romano cheese, grated
Olive oil   Salt and coarsely ground black pepper

Heat the oven to 220 C / 425 F / gas 7 and roll out the dough. Peel the shallots and slice them finely. Scatter the shallots over the dough. Sprinkle the cheese over this, moisten with a little oil and season with salt. Bake until golden brown, remove from the oven, sprinkle coarsely ground pepper over it, and serve.

26   PIZZA WITH AUBERGINE [1]

Basic dough recipe   *Fills 6 pizzas*
3 large aubergines   Salt   Olive oil
700 g / 24 oz canned tomatoes, drained and chopped
500 g / 18 oz Mozzarella cheese, thinly sliced
Oregano   Freshly ground black pepper

First prepare the aubergine. Cut off the stalk end, halve the eggplant, remove the pulp and seeds and cut the flesh with its skin into small cubes. Put the cubes into

a colander, salt well and leave for 1 hour or more. Rinse and dry the cubes. Heat the oven to 220 C/425 F/gas 7. Fry the cubes in plenty of oil, stirring, until golden on all sides. Drain the cubes and salt them lightly. Roll out the pizza dough. On each circle spread a generous amount of the tomato pulp forced through a sieve. Scatter the aubergine, Mozzarella slices, a pinch of oregano and pepper on top. Moisten with oil and bake until the crust is golden.

Another version adds chopped black olives to the filling.

27　PIZZA WITH AUBERGINE [2]

This recipe is similar to the preceding one. Instead of sautéing the aubergine in a lot of oil, use only a small amount and add tomato pulp, 2–3 garlic cloves, sliced, and finally a pinch of oregano and about 100 ml/4 oz stoned and chopped olives. When the ingredients are cooked, about 10 minutes, spread the mixture over the dough, cover with the Mozzarella and, if wished, 4 skinned, seeded tomato halves, moisten with a little oil and bake.

Pizza with aubergine [1]

Pizza with curly endive [2]

28   PIZZA WITH CURLY ENDIVE [1]

Basic dough recipe   *Fills 1 pizza*
$\frac{1}{2}$ head of curly endive   3 anchovy fillets, washed and chopped
Olive oil   30 ml/2 tbls capers   45 ml/3 tbls chopped black or green olives
Heat the oven to 220 C/425 F/gas 7 and roll out the dough a little over 4 mm/ $\frac{1}{8}$ in thick. Clean and parboil the endive, drain and cut it into strips. Heat a few tablespoons of oil in a frying-pan and brown the endive with the anchovy, the capers and olives. Cook for about 10 minutes, stirring occasionally. Pour the mixture over the dough and bake until the dough is golden.

29   PIZZA WITH CURLY ENDIVE [2]

Add 12 g/$\frac{1}{2}$ oz pine nuts and 12 g/$\frac{1}{2}$ oz raisins, first revived in a little hot water and drained, to the frying-pan with the mixture in the preceding recipe. The raisins and pine nuts can be added after the mixture is spread over the dough. Sprinkle over 30 ml/2 tbls grated Parmesan cheese and bake. This recipe was suggested to me by Franco Simeone, a pizzamaker of the Bruschetta restaurant in Milan.

30   PIZZA WITH ARTICHOKES [1]

Basic dough recipe   *Fills 1 pizza*
1 large artichoke per person   Salt and freshly ground black pepper
175 g/6 oz Mozzarella cheese, thinly sliced   Lemon juice
Remove the artichokes' tough outer leaves and chokes. Cut the rest into thin slices. Immediately put them into lemon juice and water to cover so they don't turn colour. Heat the oven to 220 C/425 F/gas 7 and roll out the dough. Drain and spread the artichoke hearts over the dough, add the Mozzarella slices, season with salt and pepper and bake in the hot oven until the crust is golden and the cheese has melted. You can substitute any other soft cheese for the Mozzarella.

Pizza with artichokes [1]

31 PIZZA WITH ARTICHOKES [2]

Basic dough recipe   *Fills 1 pizza*
1 large artichoke   Olive oil
1–2 garlic cloves per person, crushed but whole
1 anchovy fillet, washed and mashed
45 ml / 3 tbls finely chopped black olives
7.5 ml / 1½ tsp capers, chopped   Freshly ground black pepper
7.5 ml / 1½ tsp chopped parsley

Prepare the artichoke heart as in recipe **30**. Heat the oven to 220 C / 425 F / gas 7 and roll out the dough. Gently heat 15 ml / 1 tbls oil in a frying-pan and add the whole crushed garlic cloves. When they have browned, remove them. Add the anchovy fillet to the oil, stirring it a little, then add the olives, the capers and finally the well-drained artichoke slices. Sprinkle with pepper and parsley. Stir frequently until the artichoke is half-cooked, then pour the mixture over the dough and bake until golden.

32 PIZZA WITH DRIED TOMATOES

Split sun-dried tomatoes come from Puglia, though they can now be found in glass jars in Italian speciality food stores. They are preserved in green olive oil flavoured with garlic, aromatic herbs and sometimes small bits of red chilli.

A secret to using them in the kitchen is to put them on a plate in a warm oven. After a few minutes they become softer and will not dry out as quickly when you then cook with them.

Basic dough recipe   *Fills 1 pizza*
Olive oil   1 small onion, chopped
1 small jar dried tomatoes, drained and softened
about 100 ml/4 fl oz tomato sauce (recipe, page **19**)

Heat the oven to 220 C/425 F/gas 7 and roll out the dough. Heat a little oil in a frying-pan with the chopped onion. Add the prepared dried tomatoes and mix well. When they are hot, remove from the heat. Cover the dough with the tomato sauce and spoon 15 ml/1 tbls of the onion and dried tomatoes on each round, moisten with more oil and bake until the dough is golden.

33 PIZZA MACEDONIA [1]

Basic dough recipe   *Fills 6 pizza*
450 g/1 lb courgettes, cut into thin rounds
450 g/1 lb tomatoes, blanched, peeled, seeded and chopped
450 g/1 lb onions, chopped   450 g/1 lb fleshy plums, stoned and chopped
450 g/1 lb green pepper, seeded and chopped   Olive oil
Salt and freshly ground black pepper

Heat the oven to 220 C/425 F/gas 7 and roll out the dough. Mix the courgettes, tomatoes, onions, plums and green pepper together in a large bowl. Slowly add a thin stream of oil to them until you get a rather solid mixture. If it is too liquid, drain off the excess moisture. Add salt and pepper and spread the mixture over the tops of the dough. Bake until the vegetables are tender and the crust is nicely browned.

34 PIZZA MACEDONIA [2]

You can vary the recipe above by substituting mangoes for the plums.

35 PIZZA MACEDONIA [3]

The pizza can be enriched by adding a fresh creamy cheese-like Ricotta or Stracchino to the vegetable and fruit mixutre, about 450 g/1 lb, and blending it in well.

36 PIZZA MACEDONIA [4]

Another excellent addition is about 100 g/4 oz canned, drained tunafish to the vegetable and fruit mixture, or adding both the cheese and the tuna. The flavours go very well together.

Macedonia pizza [1]

37 PIZZA WITH BLACK TRUFFLES

Basic dough recipe   *Fills 1 pizza*
100 ml / 4 fl oz olive oil   1–2 garlic cloves per pizza, crushed
1–2 anchovy fillets, washed and mashed   Freshly ground black pepper
2 black truffles, the size of a walnut, thinly sliced

Heat the oven to 220 C / 425 F / gas 7 and roll out the dough. Heat the oil in a frying-pan. Add the whole, crushed garlic cloves and anchovy fillets to the oil and stir occasionally. When the garlic has browned remove it and take the pan off the heat. Brush the oil mixture over the dough and sprinkle with black pepper. Cover with slices of black truffle and bake until the crust is golden.

38 PIZZA WITH WHITE TRUFFLES AND PARMESAN

Basic dough price   ·   *Fills 1 pizza*
Olive oil   About 25 g / 1 oz Parmesan cheese, coarsely grated
2 white truffles, the size of a walnut, thinly sliced

Heat the oven to 220 C / 425 F / gas 7 and roll out the dough. Heat a small amount of oil in a frying-pan, then add the cheese. Stir it so that it is coated with the oil.

Pizza with mushroom [1]

Do not let it melt. Pour this over the dough; there should be enough to cover the surface. Garnish each circle generously with white truffle slices and bake until the crust is golden.

39   PIZZA WITH MUSHROOMS [1]

Basic dough recipe   *Fills 1 pizza*
75 g / 3 oz mushrooms, cleaned   Olive oil
½ garlic clove, finely chopped   7.5 g / 1½ tsp chopped parsley

Heat the oven to 220 C / 425 F / gas 7 and roll out the dough. Cut the mushrooms into pieces or slices and sauté them in a little oil. Add the chopped garlic and parsley and cook just until the mushrooms have lost their raw appearance. Pour the mushroom mixture over the dough and bake. When the dough is golden brown, the mushrooms will be just right. Serve immediately.

40   PIZZA WITH MUSHROOMS [2]

This recipe is the same as the one above except that 30 ml / 2 tbls of blanched, peeled, seeded and sieved tomatoes or tomato sauce (page **19**) are spread over the dough before the mushrooms are added.

41   PIZZA WITH GORGONZOLA [1]

Fills 1 pizza

Basic dough recipe
150 g / 5 oz mild Gorgonzola or other
   mild blue cheese, crumbled
1–2 garlic cloves, thinly sliced or
   chopped   Olive oil

Heat the oven to 220 C / 425 F / gas 7 and roll out the dough. Spread a thin layer of crumbled Gorgonzola on the pizza dough, sprinkle the minced or sliced garlic over it, moisten with olive oil and bake until the crust is golden and the cheese has melted.

42   PIZZA WITH GORGONZOLA [2]

Instead of garlic substitute 30 ml / 2 tbls finely chopped onion and proceed as in version [1].

43   PIZZA WITH GORGONZOLA [3]

In addition to the ingredients listed in version [1], you will need 3 medium-sized tomatoes, blanched, peeled, seeded and chopped. Sprinkle the dough with crumbled Gorgonzola, then the tomatoes, and a little garlic. Moisten with olive oil and bake until the dough is golden brown and the cheese is well melted. Add salt or finely ground fresh pepper and serve. I owe this recipe to Alberto Cortesi who had me try it at the Charleston restaurant in Milan.

Pizza with Gorgonzola [1]

Three cheese pizza

44 PIZZA WITH APPLES AND RICOTTA CHEESE

You need for this pizza a very soft and rather creamy cheese like Ricotta or Stracchino.

 Basic dough recipe   *Fills 1 pizza*
 3 medium-sized sweetish apples, peeled, cored and chopped very fine
 Peeled, cored, sliced apples, to garnish (optional)
 350 g / 12 oz Ricotta, Stracchino or other mild soft cheese
 Olive oil

 Heat the oven to 220 C / 425 F / gas 7 and roll out the dough very thinly. Mix the chopped apple in with the cheese and spread it over the dough. Moisten with a little oil and bake until the crust is golden.

45 THREE CHEESE PIZZA

For each individual pizza you will need:

 Basic dough recipe   *Fills 1 pizza*
 40 g / 1½ oz Mozzarella or Scamorza cheese, grated
 40 g / 1½ oz Fontina or Gruyère cheese, grated
 40 g / 1½ oz Provolone or Pecorino cheese, grated
 Salt and freshly ground black pepper Olive oil

 Heat the oven to 220 C / 425 F / gas 7 and roll out the dough. Mix the cheeses together and distribute them over the dough, sprinkle with salt and pepper and moisten with oil. Bake until the crust is golden and the cheese is melted and slightly browned.

Pizza with apples and Ricotta

Sometimes the cheese is not grated, but shredded, mixed and then just melted a little in some butter with salt and pepper. A good trick is to dissolve 15 ml / 1 tbls flour in 30 ml / 2 tbls milk and stir this into the cheese. This helps form a creamy mass that can be poured over the pizza dough for baking.

46   FOUR CHEESE PIZZA

This recipe is the same as above except that you combine four cheeses instead of three. You can try various combinations, for example, adding Gorgonzola to the three mentioned above. Mild, soft Gorgonzola is best, since it tolerates the heat and melts well.

47   FIVE CHEESE PIZZA

Again the recipe is similar to the previous ones except for the number of cheeses. A good combination of five cheeses might be Mozzarella, Provolone, Fontina, Gruyère and Gorgonzola. But there are many possibilities including Parmesan, Caciocavallo, Pecorino or Romano.

48   PIZZA WITH MOZZARELLA OR SCAMORZA AND POTATOES

Basic dough recipe   *Fills 1 pizza*
1 small potato   Salt and coarsely ground black pepper
50 g / 2 oz Mozzarella or Scamorza cheese per person
1 anchovy fillet, rinsed and chopped   Olive oil

Heat the oven to 220 C / 425 F / gas 7 and roll out the dough. Boil the potato until just tender, then peel and cut it into thin slices. Cut the cheese into thin slices and spread the potatoes and cheese over the pizza, overlapping. On top sprinkle the anchovy pieces, moisten with the oil and sprinkle with salt and a little coarsely ground pepper. Bake until the crust is golden.

49   PIZZA WITH TALEGIO

Taleggio is a semi-soft somewhat pungent cheese made from cow's milk. You can substitute any soft, creamy cheese. You will need approximately 250 g / 9 oz of Taleggio or similar cheese per pizza, crumbled over the pizza dough, then moisten with oil and bake.

A variation which gives this pizza a richer flavour would be to add 40 g / 1½ tbls of finely chopped onion over the cheese before baking.

50   PIZZA ALLA CAPOGNA

This is an adaption for pizza of a recipe created by one of the best chefs I know, Pino Capogna.

Basic dough recipe   *Fills 1 pizza*
10–15 ml / 2–3 tsp grated fresh horseradish   30 ml / 2 tbls soybean oil
30 ml / 2 tbls wine vinegar   200 g / 7 oz Ricotta cheese
100 g / 4 oz Mascarpone or other cream cheese, mixed with a little single cream
    to soften

Heat the oven to 220 C / 425 F / gas 7 and roll out the dough. Mix the horseradish with the oil and vinegar and let it marinate for 2 hours. Discard the oil and vinegar and mix the horseradish with the Ricotta and Mascarpone or cream cheese. Mix them well to obtain a smooth and homogenous mixture, adding olive oil little by little as necessary. Spread this over the dough and bake until the crust is golden.

Pizza alla Capogna

51 PESTO PIZZA

Basic dough recipe *Fills 1 pizza*
6 basil leaves, wiped clean
1 garlic clove   Coarse salt   50 ml / 2 fl oz olive oil
15 ml / 1 tbls grated Pecorino or Parmesan cheese
15 ml / 1 tbls pine nuts (optional)

Heat the oven to 220 C / 425 F / gas 7 and roll out the dough. Crush the basil together with the garlic and a pinch of coarse salt (this helps to preserve basil's colour), then stir in the oil, little by little, till you get a well blended purée. Mix in the cheese and the pine nuts, if wished.

Moisten the pizza dough with a little oil and put it in the oven. When it is half-baked, take it out and cover it generously with the basil mixture, then put it back in to finish cooking.

Pizza with onions, Ricotta and gorgonzola

52   PIZZA WITH ONIONS, RICOTTA AND GORGONZOLA

Basic dough recipe   *Fills 6 pizzas*
3 medium-sized onions, finely chopped   350 g / 12 oz Ricotta cheese
350 g / 12 oz mild Gorgonzola or other blue cheese   Salt   Olive oil

Heat the oven to 220 C / 425 F / gas 7 and roll out the dough. Beat the onion, Ricotta and blue cheese together, adding a little salt and enough oil to bind and soften it. Cover the pizza dough with this mixture and bake until the cheese has melted and the crust is golden.

In other versions you can use milk instead of oil and you can also add finely chopped celery to either the milk or oil version.

53   PIZZA WITH CLAMS [1]

Basic dough recipe   *Fills 1 pizza*
500 g / 18 oz clams per individual pizza, cleaned
4 medium-sized tomatoes, blanched, peeled, seeded and chopped
Salt and freshly ground black pepper   Oregano

Heat the oven to 220 C / 425 F / gas 7 and roll out the dough. Place the wet clams

Pizza with clams [1]

in a saucepan over low heat and cover for 3–4 minutes. Discard any which do not open, remove the meat from the others, strain the liquid that is released and reserve the clams and liquid separately.

Spread the tomatoes over the pizza dough, sprinkle with salt, pepper and a pinch of oregano and bake until the dough has browned. Remove from the oven, cover with the clams, moisten with a little of the clam liquid and serve immediately.

54   PIZZA WITH CLAMS [2]

The recipe is the same as described above, except that the tomatoes are eliminated. The pizzas are baked simply moistened with a little oil, a sprinkling of oregano and a pinch of salt and pepper. When baked, they are garnished with the clams and served immediately.

55   PIZZA WITH MUSSELS

Because of their delicacy many people prefer mussels to clams. You will need 6 mussles per person. The procedure is exactly the same as with clams, both in the version with tomatoes and the version without. But the flavour of the tomatoes can easily predominate, so if you decide to use them, you might want to reduce the

quantity. As in the recipes using clams, when the dough has baked, garnish with the mussels and moisten with a little reserved mussel liquid.

56   PIZZA WITH MIXED SEAFOOD

This can be made with all kinds of seafood, not only those mentioned already but squid and others. Squid should be cleaned, washed, transparent 'bone' removed, and skinned, then the body cut into bite-sized rings, sautéed briefly and added with the other ingredients after baking. A good combination would be prawns, squid, mussels and clams, but any combination could work.

57   PIZZA WITH OYSTERS

This is also a recent invention. You will need 4–6 oysters per person, lemon, and the basic dough. Moisten the rolled out dough with a little oil, sprinkle with salt and bake at 220 C/425 F/gas 7 till golden brown. While it bakes, prepare the oysters. Open them, place them on a plate and gently squeeze a little lemon over them. When the dough is baked, place the oysters on top. Sprinkle a little freshly ground pepper over all, if wished.

58   PIZZA WITH FRESH ANCHOVIES

Fresh anchovies – better if they are rather small – should be well cleaned and placed on the pizza round, then sliced or chopped garlic is added. Moisten with olive oil, sprinkle with salt and pepper and bake at 220 C/425 F/gas 7.

The anchovies are even better if marinated in a little oil with garlic, salt and pepper for an hour or two (no vinegar or lemon should be used as it leaves an acidic taste). Pour the whole mixture over the pizza and bake.

59   PIZZA WITH FRESH SARDINES

The recipe is similar to Pizza with Fresh Anchovies, **58**, but in some versions sieved tomato pulp is spread over the dough before adding the well cleaned and boned sardines, either fresh or canned. You will need approximately 3–5 per person.

In other versions chopped or sliced onions can replace the garlic and you can add a pinch of oregano.

60   PIZZA WITH SQUID

Basic dough recipe   *Fills 1 pizza*
225 g/8 oz cleaned squid
1 small onion, finely chopped
45 ml/3 tbls olive oil
30 ml/2 tbls finely chopped parsley
Salt and freshly ground black pepper

Heat the oven to 220 C/425 F/gas 7 and roll out the dough. Cut the tentacles from the squid, remove the sac and inner 'bone', rub off the skin, then cut the body into rings. Gently sauté the onion in the oil until translucent but not browned, then add the parsley. Let this cook a few minutes, then stir in the squid rings, salt and pepper. Spread this mixture over the dough and bake until golden.

Pizza with mixed seafood

61 PIZZA WITH FRESH ROE

When they can be found, fresh fish eggs are like manna for any kind of cooking. For pizza, spread 30 ml/2 tbls of chopped onion per pizza over the dough, then the fish eggs and moisten with olive oil. Bake at 220 C/425 F/gas 7 until the crust is golden.

You can also gently sauté the onions in oil until translucent but not browned, then spreading them over the dough, followed by the fish eggs, before baking.

62 PIZZA WITH SEAWEED

This came from a spaghetti recipe of my friend, Emilio Regonaschi. Sea weed can occasionally be found in fish stores and should be washed well, then chopped. Mix this with twice that amount of Gorgonzola cheese and a drop of fruit brandy or grappa. Cover the pizza dough with this mixture and bake at 220 C/425 F/gas 7 until golden.

You can also add dry sea weed which can be found in some stores carrying Japanese foods. It should be soaked first in warm water.

63 PIZZA WITH APPLES AND PRAWNS

The combination of prawns and apples, which is also a classic antipasto, makes this delicious pizza.

> Basic dough recipe *Fills 1 pizza*
> 18–24 cooked, peeled small prawns, defrosted if frozen
> 3 tart green apples, cored and cut into very small cubes
> Olive oil

Heat the oven to 220 C/425 F/gas 7 and roll out the dough. Chop the prawns into small pieces. Spread the chopped apples over the circles, approximately 45 ml/3 tbls per person, then add the prawns, moisten with oil and bake until the dough is golden brown.

64 PIZZA WITH SMOKED HERRING

Smoked herring, cleaned and coarsely chopped, takes the place of salted anchovies in this recipe for Roman-style pizza.

> Basic dough recipe *Fills 6 pizzas*
> 350 g/12 oz smoked herrings, cleaned and coarsely chopped
> Milk
> 6–8 medium-sized tomatoes, blanched, peeled, seeded and cut in wedges
> 500 g/18 oz Mozzarella cheese, sliced
> Olive oil
> Coarsely ground black pepper

Soak the chopped herring in milk to cover for a few hours, so it will be less salty. Meanwhile, heat the oven to 220 C/425 F/gas 7 and roll the dough out thinly. When the herring is ready, spread the dough with the tomatoes, then the Mozzarella, and finally the pieces of herring, drained, omitting the basil which usually accompanies a Roman-style pizza. Moisten with olive oil and bake until the crust is golden and the tomatoes are soft. When it is done, sprinkle with coarsely ground pepper.

65 PIZZA WITH SMOKED EEL

The recipe is the same as described in Pizza with Smoked Herring **64**, but smoked eels are substituted for the herring.

Pizza with seaweed

66   PIZZA WITH SMOKED SALMON

Pizza with smoked salmon

Basic dough recipe   *Fills 1 pizza*
125–225 g / $\frac{1}{4}$–$\frac{1}{2}$ lb smoked salmon, cut into small pieces
1 small onion, finely chopped   Dried mint   Olive oil

Heat the oven to 220 C / 425 F / gas 7 and roll out the dough thinly. Spread the smoked salmon and chopped onion, mixing them a little, on the dough. Sprinkle over a little dried mint and moisten with oil. Bake until the crust is golden.

It is better to be stingy with the onion than to put too much, so its flavour does not dominate the salmon.

67   PIZZA WITH CAVIAR

This is quite expensive of course, but extraordinary if you try it. Generously spread the caviar and a little chopped onion over a very thin round of dough, sprinkle with a tablespoon of finely chopped parsley, moisten with oil and bake at 220 C / 425 F / gas 7 till the crust is golden.

68   PIZZA WITH RED CAVIAR

The recipe is the same as the one for pizza with classic caviar, but you can, if it pleases your palate, add a bit more onion.

Pizza with tuna [1]

69 PIZZA WITH TUNA [1]

Basic dough recipe
30 ml/2 tbls good quality canned tuna, drained
1 medium-sized onion, chopped
Basil leaves, wiped clean
Olive oil

Fills 1 pizza

Heat the oven to 220 C/425 F/gas 7 and roll out the dough. Crumble the tuna in a bowl. Mix in the onion and spread it over the rounds of dough. Garnish with a few fresh basil leaves, moisten with a little oil and bake until the crust is golden.

70 PIZZA WITH TUNA [2]

The recipe is the same as **69**, but you can add about 15 ml/1 tbls chopped black or green olives or chopped celery to the tuna before baking.

71 PIZZA WITH TUNA [3]

This recipe is similar to the preceding ones with tuna. In this version, add 75 g/3 oz chopped celery to the crumbled tuna and omit the other ingredients. Spread it on the dough and moisten with a little oil and bake.

72 PIZZA WITH TUNA [4]

Gently sauté 1 small chopped onion in 30 ml/2 tbls olive oil until translucent but not browned. Add one tomato, chopped, and let this cook together a few minutes. Add the drained, canned tuna, stirring a little to break it up. Spread this over the dough and bake at 220 C/425 F/gas 7 until the crust is golden brown.

You can also add 15 ml/1 tbls chopped celery or 5 ml/1 tsp chopped capers.

73 PIZZA WITH TUNA AND RICOTTA

Basic dough recipe   *Fills 1 pizza*
30 ml/2 tbls good quality canned tuna, drained well
100 g/4 oz Ricotta cheese   Olive oil
Onion juice (grated and sieved onion)   Freshly ground black pepper

Heat the oven to 220 C/425 F/gas 7 and roll out the dough. Work the tuna and Ricotta together until they are well mixed, then little by little, add enough oil so that you have a smooth mixture. Add onion juice and pepper to taste. Cover the pizza dough with this mixture and bake until golden.

74 PIZZA WITH *BOTTARGA*

Bottarga are dried fish eggs which come from a particular fish found in Italy. They are pressed and dried in the sun and end up looking a little like salami. Tuna *bottarga* also exists; it is saltier but also appetizing. Smoked cod's roe could be substituted.

For the pizza, sprinkle the dough with chopped onion, some grated *bottarga* or cod's roe, moisten with olive oil and bake at 220 C/425 F/gas 7 till the crust is golden.

You can also cover the dough with slices of Mozzarella, then the *bottarga* or cod's roe, moisten with the oil and bake.

75 PIZZA WITH SNAILS

Basic dough recipe   *Fills 1 pizza*
6 or more canned or fresh commercially cultivated snails
Coarse salt
Dry white wine
1 small onion, finely chopped
1 small tomato, blanched, peeled, seeded and finely chopped
45 ml/3 tbls olive oil

If using fresh snails, boil them in water for 15 minutes, drain them and take them out of their shells. Then cut off the black tail-like piece which has a bad flavour. Clean them with tepid water, drain, then cover them with coarse salt moistened with 30 ml/2 tbls of the wine for 1 hour. Wash the snails and wipe them with a cloth to remove any trace of mucus. Then marinate them for 1 hour in 100 ml/3½ fl oz of the wine. Finally wash them well in a colander under running water, stirring occasionally.

Heat the oven to 220 C/425 F/gas 7 and roll out the dough. Gently sauté the onion and tomato in the oil with a sprinkling of salt and pepper. Simmer the snails briefly in 50 ml/2 fl oz white wine. Drain and chop the snails and add them to the onion mixture. Cover the dough with this mixture and bake until the snails are ready and the dough is golden.

Pizza with snails

76   PIZZA WITH PROSCIUTTO [1]

The difficulty in preparing this pizza, which is liked by so many, especially in northern Italy, is that thinly sliced prosciutto – Italian 'raw' (salted and cured) ham – dries out when baked at high temperatures. Thus it is a good idea to use slightly thicker slices and cut them into small strips which include some of the fatty part, if possible.

> Basic dough recipe   *Fills 6 pizzas*
> 350 g / 12 oz prosciutto, thinly sliced, or thin slices of fatty cooked ham
> 500 g / 18 oz Mozzarella cheese, cubed or sliced
> Olive oil

Heat the oven to 220 C / 425 F / gas 7 and roll out the dough. Arrange the ham on the dough, cover with the Mozzarella and moisten with a little oil. Bake in the hot oven until the crust is golden and the cheese has melted.

77   PIZZA WITH PROSCIUTTO [2]

In this version, you can substitute Fontina or Bel Paese cheese or another soft cheese for the Mozzarella in recipe **76**, then add 225 g / 8 oz chopped black or green olives.

Pizza with prosciutto [1]

78   PIZZA WITH POTATOES AND SAUSAGE

Basic dough recipe   *Fills 1 pizza*
3 small potatoes   175 g / 6 oz fresh pork sausage
Salt   Olive oil

Heat the oven to 220 C / 425 F / gas 7 and roll out the dough. Boil the potatoes until tender, then peel and cut them into slices. Crumble the sausage or cut it into rounds. Put a layer of potatoes over the dough, moisten with a little oil, sprinkle with salt and garnish with the sausage. Moisten with a little more oil and bake until the crust is golden and the sausage has cooked.

79   PIZZA WITH *COTECHINO* AND EGG SAUCE

Cotechino sausages are fresh, coarsely ground pork sausages with a thick skin. They are usually about 20 cm / 8 in long and 6.5 cm / 2½ in in diameter. They can be substituted with any other fresh, coarsely ground pork sausage.

Basic dough recipe   *Fills 1 pizza*
100 g / 4 oz *cotechino* or other pork sausage   175 g / 6 oz Ricotta
2 medium-sized eggs   25 g / 1 oz good quality canned tuna, well drained
Olive oil   Lemon juice

Pizza with potatoes and sausage

Heat the oven to 220C/425F/gas7 and roll out the dough. Simmer the sausage for about 30 minutes. Cut in slices, neither very thick nor very thin; remove the skin. Spread the cheese generously over the dough and put the sausage slices on top. Bake until the crust is golden.

Meanwhile, prepare a sauce by beating the eggs and the tuna together, adding oil till the mixture is creamy. At the end add a few drops of lemon juice. When the pizza is cooked cover it with the sauce. Remove the pizzas from the oven. The heat should cause the eggs to set. Serve immediately.

80 PIZZA ALLA CRISTOFORO

This pizza was the idea of Cristoforo Adesini, a pizza lover and the owner of a place in Milan, in the via Napo Torriani, where pizza makers and other friends get together for experiments which often are brilliant.

Fills 6 pizzas

Basic dough recipe
500 g/18 oz Mozzarella cheese
175 ml/6 fl oz thick tomato sauce
  (recipe, page **19**)
350 g/12 oz Pecorino or Romano
  cheese, grated
1 pepperoni sausage, thinly sliced
About 50 thin asparagus tips, cooked
  al dente (firm yet tender)
Basil leaves, wiped clean
Olive oil

Heat the oven to 220C/425F/gas7. Roll out the dough very thinly, so it will become crispy when it is baked. Cover it with thin slices of Mozzarella that will melt completely during cooking, then 15–30 ml/1–2 tbls tomato sauce per pizza and sprinkle the grated cheese over it. Garnish with sausage slices, about 10 per pizza, the asparagus tips, dividing them among the six circles, and the basil leaves. Moisten each one with oil and

bake until the dough is crisp and golden.

One often eats pizza with many good ingredients, but too many don't work. This pizza, although it is very rich, has ingredients which go together very well. It can really serve as a complete meal.

81   PIZZA WITH PANCETTA

Pancetta is fatty bacon–like roll as seen on page **64**. Thinly sliced streaky bacon can be substituted although the flavour will not be the same.

Fills 6 pizzas

Basic dough recipe
450 g / 1 lb *pancetta* or streaky bacon, thinly sliced
350 g / 12 oz Pecorino or Romano cheese, grated
Olive oil

Heat the oven to 220 C / 425 F / gas 7 and roll out the dough. Cut the *pancetta* or bacon to separate the fat from the lean. Chop the fat very finely and cut the lean into small pieces. Scatter the fat over the base of the circle first so that it forms a very thin layer covering the bottom, leaving a small margin around the edge. On top, distribute the lean part evenly and then sprinkle with the cheese, moisten with oil and bake until the crust is golden and the pizza is cooked through.

Pizza alla Christoforo

82 PIZZA WITH PANCETTA [2]

This is a slightly more elaborate version.

Basic dough recipe   *Fills 6 pizzas*
450 g / 1 lb *pancetta* or streaky bacon   Olive oil   425 g / 15 oz chopped onions
225 g / 8 oz tomatoes, blanched, peeled, seeded and chopped, or canned
    tomatoes, drained and chopped
Salt and freshly ground black pepper

Heat the oven to 220 C / 425 F / gas 7 and roll out the dough. Cut the *pancetta* or bacon in small cubes. Put a very little oil in a frying-pan and add the *pancetta*. Let it brown a little, then drain and keep warm. Meanwhile in another pan, sauté the onions in a little oil until they are translucent, then add the tomato pulp or canned tomatoes, salt and pepper and let this cook gently for a few minutes. Finally pour it over the dough, sprinkle with the *pancetta* and bake until the crust is golden.

Other versions add chopped black or green olives.

83 PIZZA ALLA FRANCO

This is an original creation of Franco Genna, a Sicilian pizza-maker living in Milan.

Basic dough recipe   *Fills 6 pizzas*
900 g / 2 lb Mozzarella cheese, cut in slices
90 ml / 6 tbls of a good quality sharp mustard
350 g / 12 oz *pancetta* or streaky bacon, cut into cubes

Heat the oven to 220 C / 425 F / gas 7. Roll out the dough into thin circles. Arrange the slices of Mozzarella over each one, then spread a spoonful of the mustard on each, scatter the *pancetta* or streaky bacon on top, moisten with oil and bake until the crust is browned.

84 PIZZA WITH CHICKEN LIVERS

Basic dough recipe   *Fills 1 pizza*
225 g / 8 oz chicken livers   Olive oil   25 g / 1 oz chopped parsley
1–2 garlic cloves per person, sliced   Salt and freshly ground black pepper

Heat the oven to 220 C / 425 F / gas 7 and roll out the dough. Clean the chicken livers and cut them into small pieces. Sauté them briefly in a little oil with the garlic, salt and pepper. Pour this over the dough, sprinkle the parsley over them and bake until the dough is crisp. Coarsely grind black pepper over all and serve right away.

85 PIZZA WITH TRIPE

Basic dough recipe   *Fills 6 pizzas*
450 g / 1 lb tripe, partially cooked
350 g / 12 fl oz tomato sauce (recipe, page **19**)
175 g / 6 oz Parmesan or Romano cheese, grated

Heat the oven to 220 C / 425 F / gas 7 and roll out the dough. Clean and wash the tripe and boil until tender. Drain, then cut it into rather short strips. Heat the tomato sauce and add the tripe, letting it cook for 2–3 minutes. Cover the dough with this mixture, sprinkle over the grated cheese and bake until the crust is browned.

Pizza with pancetta [2]

86 PIZZA WITH PROSCIUTTO AND FIGS

Basic dough recipe   *Fills 6 pizzas*
24 ripe figs, cut into pieces, stems discarded   Olive oil
225 g/8 oz prosciutto or fatty cooked ham, thinly sliced

Heat the oven to 220 C/425 F/gas 7. Roll out the dough into thin circles. Arrange a layer of figs over them and then the prosciutto, cut into strips containing both fat and lean meat. Moisten with oil and bake until the dough is golden.

This may seem like a strange combination, but figs were often used in sauces in the past with good results. Try it.

87 PIZZA WITH PEPPERS AND FIGS

Again, figs on pizza and in cooking. I mentioned above that they were common in olden days. The Latin writer, Apicius, for example, who left us the only more or less complete Roman cookery book, gives recipes where figs were part of sauces and stews, often replacing onions. A famous recipe in ancient Rome was *jecur ficatum*, which was liver (*jecur*) with figs, a dish in which the figs were sautéed in a little oil and strips of liver, herbs and spices. The name of this dish was eventually shortened to *ficatum* and you can imagine Julius Caesar returning home in the evening for dinner and his wife meeting him with a smile, saying 'My darling, I've made *ficatum* for you just the way you like it'. Today, the Italian word for liver is *fegato* and the word *jecur* has been lost.

History aside, for the pizza with peppers and figs, you will need:

Basic dough recipe   *Fills 6 pizzas*
4 medium-sized green peppers, seeded and chopped   Olive oil
24 ripe figs cut into pieces, stems discarded

Heat the oven to 220 C/425 F/gas 7 and roll out the dough. Spread the green peppers over the dough, moisten with a little oil and then garnish with the figs. Bake until the crust is golden.

To vary the flavour a little you can add a little chopped celery with the peppers.

88 PIZZA AL RAGU

I owe this idea to the artist Angelo Cattaneo who does very elegant abstract works but in the kitchen remains very close to the traditional methods of his native Cremona. This pizza calls for a very fresh *ragu*, or meat-vegetable sauce, with more vegetables than meat.

Basic dough recipe   *Fills 1 pizza*
60 ml/4 tbls olive oil
1 medium-sized onion, chopped
2 celery stalks, chopped
1 large carrot, finely chopped
175 g/6 oz minced beef

Heat the oven to 220 G/425 F/gas 7 and roll out the dough. Heat the oil and add the chopped onion. Cook till it becomes translucent, then add the celery, carrots, salt and pepper. Let them cook a few minutes and add the beef. Let it brown, stirring, then divide this among the six pizza circles. Moisten with a little oil and bake until the crust is golden.

For a red version, add 1 medium-sized tomato, blanched, peeled, seeded and sieved to the ragu after you add the meat.

Pizza with peppers and figs

89   FOUR SEASONS PIZZA [1]

Basic dough recipe   *Fills 1 pizza*

½ garlic clove, sliced   2–4 anchovy fillets, washed

30 ml / 2 tbls black olives, stoned and chopped

75–100 g / 3–4 oz clams or other seafood, per person (prepared as in Pizza
  with Clams [1], recipe **53**)

1 small tomato, blanched, peeled, seeded and chopped, per person

30 ml / 2 tbls grated Mozzarella cheese   Olive oil

Heat the oven to 220 C / 425 F / gas 7. Cut off a small section from the dough before
you roll it out. You will use this to make two cords for each pizza, which will cross
and divide it into four sections on top. In each section, put different ingredients,
taking care that none of the ingredients clash with each other. For example, in one

quarter you might put garlic, anchovies and a little oil, in another, black olives, oil and anchovies, in the third quarter, the clams and in the last quarter, tomatoes, Mozzarella and again anchovies. Bake until the crust is golden.

90   FOUR SEASONS PIZZA [2]

This is identical to the one above, except that in the first section you put clams, in the second quarter you put Mozzarella and tomatoes, in the third, garlic, anchovies and oil, and in the fourth, artichoke hearts preserved in oil or frozen and cooked (in that case, drain and moisten them with a little oil for the pizza), or a mixture of chopped vegetables in oil.

91   FOUR SEASONS PIZZA [3]

All kinds of pizzas can be made using the methods described in recipe **89**. Other ideas are Mozzarella and tomato in one section, mushrooms in another, olives and capers in a third and in the last, crumbled fresh sausage, ham or prosciutto mixed with small cubes of Mozzarella.

92   PIZZA WITH PLANTAINS

This recipe was born in South America where the Italian pizza has been successfully adapted to local products.

Basic dough recipe   *Fills 1 pizza*
Lard or oil
4 small, preferably green plantains

Heat the oven to 220 C / 425 F / gas 7 and roll out the dough very thinly. Brush it with a light film of lard or oil. Cut the plantains into thin slices and flatten them a little with a wooden spatula. Sauté the slices in a little oil, just like potatoes. Drain, then cover the dough with a generous layer of plantain slices and bake until the crust is golden.

93   PIZZA WITH RED CURRANTS

Substitute red currants, stalks removed, in this recipe for the pineapple in the next 2 recipes. Then follow the directions for the recipe you prefer.

94   PIZZA WITH PINEAPPLE

This recipe was also created in South America by Italian pizza-makers looking for recipes to satisfy local taste. It is rather sweet but still pleasing. I owe the recipe to my friend, Antonio Primicera.

Basic dough recipe
1 medium-sized fresh pineapple, peeled, cored and cut into tiny pieces or
    crushed
Palm oil

Heat the oven to 220 C / 425 F / gas 7. Roll out the dough so that it is very thin, spread a generous amount of fresh pineapple over it, moisten with palm oil and bake until golden.

Four seasons pizza [1]

Pizza with pineapple and gorgonzola

95 PIZZA WITH PINEAPPLE AND GORGONZOLA

In this version spread the fresh pineapple over the thin dough, then mix in soft, crumbled Gorgonzola cheese and moisten with olive oil. Bake until golden. The pineapple and Gorgonzola form a very elegant sweet–sour taste.

96 PIZZA WITH STRAWBERRIES

In this recipe you can substitute hulled strawberries for the pineapple and follow recipe **94** or **95**. Be sure that the strawberries are not too ripe.

97 PIZZA WITH AVOCADO

The avocado is another exotic fruit whose flesh can be used in place of the pineapple. Avocado, however, has a rather mild flavour and needs to be livened up. You might mix it with the currants or strawberries, for example.

98 PIZZA WITH HEARTS OF PALM

Sprinkle chopped onions and pieces of hearts of palm over the dough, moisten with olive oil, add salt and pepper and bake. For a red version you can put blanched, peeled, seeded and chopped tomatoes on the dough first, then add the other ingredients.

99 PIZZA WITH WALNUTS OR HAZELNUTS

Typically Stracchino or Mascarpone are the cheeses eaten with nuts in Italy.

Basic dough recipe   *Fills 6 pizzas*
75–100 g / 3–4 oz walnuts or hazelnuts, chopped
150 g / 5 oz Mascarpone, Stracchino or cream cheese to which a little single cream is added
Vegetable oil

Heat the oven to 220 C / 425 F / gas 7 and roll out the dough. Mix the nuts with the cheese, moisten the dough with oil and spread the cheese and nut mixture over it. Add a little more oil and bake until the crust is golden.

100 PIZZA WITH SPAGHETTI

This may seem like a truly extravagent idea, but when my friend, Emilio Regonaschi, presented it as a tribute at a large international gathering of pizza-makers, it met with great success.

Basic dough recipe   *Fills 6 pizzas*
Olive oil or lard
350 g / 12 oz fresh spaghetti
Spaghetti sauce: tomato, ragu or clam, as preferred

Heat the oven to 220 C / 425 F / gas 7. Roll out the dough and brush it with a little lard or oil. Meanwhile have a pot of boiling water ready for the spaghetti. Just after you put the dough into the oven, add the spaghetti to the boiling water. It should be half-cooked when the pizza is nearly ready. Drain the spaghetti, and toss in a sauce of your choice. It using dried spaghetti, let it boil about 4 minutes before putting the dough in the oven.

Divide the spaghetti over the pizza circles just before the dough is completely cooked and put it back in the oven for no more than 2–3 minutes. Remember that the heat of the oven is much greater than the pot of boiling water, and 2–3 minutes is enough for the pasta and the pizza dough to finish cooking and blend their flavours and aromas.

This is truly an extravagance but a rather pleasing one. Actually it is not a very new invention. The great comic actor, Gilberto Govi, loved and always ordered it at a local pizzeria in Imperia, a town on the west coast near Genoa. Some of the details may be slightly different, but the recipe is basically the same.

101 CALZONE

Calzone is most probably the natural evolution of the pizza. The circle is more generously filled and then folded over and the edges are pressed together to keep the filling inside. This also makes it easier to eat.

You can use either regular bread dough for calzone or to make enough for six servings, you will need:

> 400 g / 14 oz preferably strong flour, or plain flour   Pinch of salt
> 20 g / $\frac{3}{4}$ oz fresh yeast or 10 g / $\frac{1}{3}$ oz dried active baking yeast, dissolved in a little lukewarm water   30 ml / 2 tbls olive oil

Make a mound of flour on a pastry board and make a well in the centre. Pour the dissolved yeast into the well and mix together, pulling in the flour from the edges. Add the oil and knead together, adding just enough water to form a soft, consistent dough. Let this rest on a cloth for at least 1 hour. Knead the dough until it is smooth and elastic and can be easily rolled out.

> 300 g / 11 oz Ricotta cheese   *Fills 6 calzones*
> 150 g / 5 oz Mozzarella cheese, cubed
> 150 g / 5 oz salami, prosciutto or ham, cut into 12 m / $\frac{1}{2}$ in cubes
> 45 ml / 3 tbls Pecorino or Romano cheese, grated
> 2–3 medium-sized eggs plus extra for brushing

Heat the oven to 200 C / 400 F / gas 6. Mix these ingredients together. If they are too dry add a little more egg white. Then divide the dough into six parts and roll each one out into a circle about 3 mm / $\frac{1}{8}$ in thick. Divide the filling among the circles, placing it on one half of it. Fold the empty side over and press the edges together. Paint the surface with a little beaten egg and carefully transfer them to a greased baking sheet. Bake until golden.

102 POOR MAN'S CALZONE

The poor man's version is still popular in southern Italy.

> Calzone dough, recipe **101**   300 g / 11 oz Ricotta cheese   *Fills 6 calzones*
> 1.4 kg / 3 lb fresh spinach or spring greens, trimmed and washed
> 75 g / 3 oz black olives, stoned and chopped   Salt
> Large pinch of cayenne pepper   Olive oil

Boil the greens briefly, drain and chop them well. Sauté it briefly in a little oil with the olives, salt, and red pepper. Mix in the Ricotta and proceed as in recipe **101**. Other versions add a few thin slices of soft cheese, like Mozzarella.

103 CALZONE, THE OLD-FASHIONED WAY

In this traditional version the stuffing is made with Ricotta and greens – spinach, beet spinach or whatever you like, prepared as in the previous recipe. When the boiled, chopped greens are put in the frying pan, 75 g / 3 oz raisins, first revived in a little warm water and drained, are added with 75 g / 3 oz pine nuts.

104 CALZONE WITH *COTECHINO* SAUCE

This version is from the Emilia region and it has recently become popular. Make a filling with 500 g / 18 oz Mozzarella, cubed, 225 g / 8 oz of *cotechino* or other coarsely ground fresh pork sausage, cooked as in recipe **79**, then skinned and chopped, and 3 beaten eggs. Proceed as in recipe **101**.

Calzone

105   CALZONE WITH FISH

This stuffing is made with fish such as sardines, fresh anchovies or mackerel, which are first cleaned, then floured and fried in a little oil. They are then drained well on absorbent paper, chopped well, moistened with more oil and a little chopped parsley is added. You could also use various, less oily fish, fresh or canned, mixed together, or seafood. You will need about 350 g / 12 oz fresh fish or 225 g / 8 oz canned, drained fish. Be sure to chop them well before mixing. Proceed as in recipe **101**.

106   GREEN CALZONE

This is jokingly called 'green' calzone because it is filled with greens, but it can also be filled with vegetables of other colours. The usual fillings are either spinach, beet spinach, batavia, courgettes, onions, peppers or whatever you have.

They should weigh a total of 300 g / 11 oz altogether for six calzones. They are first cleaned, boiled, chopped and then sautéed briefly with a little oil, salt, pepper and chopped parsley. They should remain on the crisp side. Drain them well and mix with 150 g / 5 oz crumbled fresh cheese, such as Ricotta or cottage cheese. You can also add a few tablespoons of grated Parmesan cheese. Add just enough oil to bind the mixture well, then fill the circles of dough, seal and bake as in the master recipe **101**.

107   CALZONE WITH ONIONS

This filling is made with a large amount of onions. For six people you will need:

Calzone dough, recipe **101**

900 g / 2 lb onions, chopped or sliced   Olive oil

6 anchovy fillets, washed and dried

350 g / 12 oz tomatoes, blanched, peeled, seeded and chopped, or canned, drained, chopped tomatoes   Salt and freshly ground black pepper

100 g / 4 oz Pecorino or Romano cheese, grated

Heat the oven to 200 C / 400 F / gas 6 and roll out the dough. Sauté the onions in oil until golden with the anchovies and tomatoes. Season with salt and pepper. When thoroughly mixed and well cooked, remove the mixture from the heat and add the cheese. Fill the six calzone circles as in recipe **101**, moistening each one with a little oil before folding them over. Bake until golden.

You can also add 50 g / 2 oz of raisins, soaked in warm water to revive them, but in this case it is better to omit the cheese. Alternatively, you can add 50 g / 2 oz Parmesan to the Pecorino or Romano, mixing them together before adding them to the other ingredients.

108 CALZONE WITH BATAVIA

Green calzone

Calzone dough, recipe **101**   *Fills 6 calzones*

600 g / 1¼ lb batavia   4 anchovy fillets, washed, dried and chopped
90 ml / 6 tbls olive oil   2–3 whole garlic cloves, crushed
30–45 ml / 2–3 tbls capers   100 g / 4 oz black olives, stoned and chopped

Heat the oven to 220 C / 425 F / gas 7 and roll out the dough. Heat the oil and brown the crushed garlic cloves. Remove them, add the anchovy pieces to the pan and set aside. Clean, boil and cut the curly endive into strips. Put the oil and anchovies back on the heat and add the curly endive, the capers and the olives and stir briefly. Fill the calzone with this mixture and bake according to the recipe **101**.

109
SCHIACCIATE [1]

This is a pitta-like bread and is made with a similar dough as for pizza.

400 g / 14 oz preferably strong white flour, or plain flour   Pinch of salt
25 g / 1 oz fresh yeast or 12 g / $\frac{1}{2}$ oz active dried yeast, dissolved in a little lukewarm water   Olive oil
Coarse salt, for sprinkling
Fresh rosemary leaves

Work together the flour and pinch of salt, then the dissolved yeast. Add enough water to make a soft pliable dough. Let it rest in a bowl in a cool (not cold) place for 30 minutes, covered with a damp tea-towel. Heat the oven to 220 C / 425 F / gas 7. Divide the dough into six portions and roll it out into 6 very thin circles about 10 cm / 4 in wide. Moisten each one with a little oil and bake. When the schiacciate turn golden and are just barely cooked, brush them with a little more oil and sprinkle them with coarse salt and a few rosemary leaves and put them back in the oven for a few more minutes.

Instead of rosemary you can use oregano or other herbs.

110   SCHIACCIATE [2]

This recipe is similar to the previous one, but let the dough rise about 1 hour. Put the circles in the oven without moistening them with any oil. The dough will inflate even more and as such serves as a good accompaniment for salamis and other antipasto as a kind of hot, light, flavourful bread.

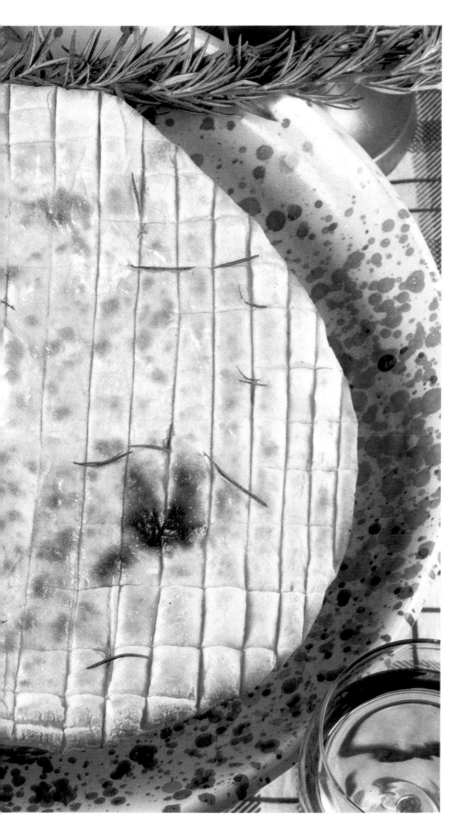

Schiacciate [*1*]

PART TWO

Frittelle, crostate, focacce and torte' rustiche

Frittelle are fritters, Italian-style, that include different doughs with or without tasty fillings like chopped anchovies, smoked salmon or cheese. *Crostate* are savoury tarts made with a delicate butter dough, while *focacce* are pies with a thin upper crust, filled with good things like tomatoes, onions and ham. *Torte rustiche* are country quiches from different regions in Italy. Also included in this section are specially flavoured, sautéed breads, baked thick dough mixtures and bread sticks.

111   MARROW BLOSSOM FRITTERS

500 g / 18 oz plain flour   Pinch of salt   *Serves 6*
20 g / ¾ oz brewers yeast dissolved in 225 ml / 8 fl oz water
300 g / 11 oz marrow blossoms
Freshly ground black pepper   Olive or other vegetable oil

Pour the flour into a bowl and add the salt. Stir the dissolved yeast into the flour, a little at a time. Add more water until you have a very thick, just fluid batter. Let this rest for an hour, covered with a cloth.

Meanwhile, prepare the marrow blossoms. Clean them first, then cut them into thin strips. When the batter has rested, it will have risen slightly but remain very thick, almost sticky. Add the marrow blossoms to it. Season with salt and papper.

Now heat about 5 cm / 2 in olive oil in a small saucepan. When it is very hot, drop a few spoonfuls of batter into the oil. They will puff up and become golden brown, delicious and delicate. Drain and cook the rest. Serve warm.

112   MOZZARELLA FRITTERS

Make up the previous batter recipe. Instead of marrow blossoms, mix in 225 g / 8 oz of Mozzarella, Scamorza or any similar cheese, cut in tiny pieces, to the batter.

Mozzarella fritters

Anchovy fritters

113 ANCHOVY FRITTERS

The recipe is identical to recipe **111** except that you add tiny pieces of washed and dried and chopped anchovy fillets to the batter.

114 SMOKED SALMON FRITTERS

In this version add bits of smoked salmon to the batter.

115 SMOKED HERRING FRITTERS

Follow recipe **111**, but add chopped smoked herring instead of marrow blossoms.

116 SMOKED EEL FRITTERS

This time add pieces of smoked eel to the batter.

117 FISH AND MOZZARELLA FRITTERS

Mix chopped anchovy or other salted and rinsed or smoked fish fillets and small Mozzarella cheese cubes together to form small balls. Dip in the batter and fry.

118 TOMATOES AND VEGETABLE FRITTERS

Follow recipe **111** for the batter. Add blanched, peeled, seeded and chopped tomatoes, mixed with chopped celery or thick matchsticks of courgettes.

119   TOMATOES, ANCHOVIES AND MOZZARELLA FRITTERS.

Add blanched, peeled, seeded and chopped tomatoes, pieces of washed and dried anchovies, and Mozzarella cheese, all cut into tiny pieces and mixed, to the batter. Prepare according to recipe **111**.

120   FRIED GNOCCO, REGGIO-STYLE

This is simply rich, fried dough. For six people, you will need:

    400 g / 14 oz plain flour
    25 g / 1 oz brewer's yeast dissolved in
      a little water
    200 g / 7 oz soft lard
    Pinch of salt
    Lard for frying

Make a dough by mixing the flour, the dissolved yeast, the softened lard and a pinch of salt. Knead well. You should get a soft, smooth, consistent dough. Let this rest for an hour under a cloth. It will rise a little.

Roll it out to a thickness of 3 mm / $\frac{1}{8}$ in and cut it into diamond shapes. Fry these diamonds in a pan with plenty of very hot lard, then drain them well on absorbent paper.

They are delicious as they are, as an accompaniment to salami, prosciutto, ham or cheese, or curly endive, or with radishes sautéed in a little butter with 1–2 slices of garlic.

Fried gnocco, Reggio-style

121   CRESCENTINE

These are almost the same as the fried gnocco but they are called crescentine in Bologna. They are a bit thicker and cut in circles instead of diamonds. You can add bits of chopped ham or prosciutto to the dough, fry them, then serve them sprinkled with more chopped ham or prosciutto, if wished.

122   CHISOLINI

These are part of the *gnocco* and the *crescentine* family. They come from Mantua. For six people you need:

400 g / 14 oz plain flour
Large pinch of salt
125 g / 1 oz yeast dissolved in a little
    water
50 g / 2 oz butter, at room temperature
50 ml / 2 tbls milk
Olive or other vegetable oil or lard

Make a dough combining the flour, a pinch of salt, and the yeast dissolved in water. Let this rest a little, then work in the butter, and finally the milk to get a rather soft but consistent dough.

Pull off small pieces of the dough and flatten them into diamond-shaped pieces about 3 mm / $\frac{1}{8}$ in thick. Fry them in plenty of oil or lard. They should puff up a little during cooking. Turn them over as they cook so that both sides turn a golden brown. Eat these as an accompaniment to cheese, prosciutto, ham or salami.

Crescentine

123 BURT-LENA

This is a version of fried dough still made in the Piacenza area going towards the Appenines. The dough and the cooking are the same as for fried gnocco, recipe **120**, but the dough is a bit thinner.

124 FRIED PIZZA [1]

These are circles of dough on which a filling is spread on half and the other side is folded over it, like a small calzone. The main difference between them is that calzone is baked and these little pizzas are fried. For six people, you will need:

400 g / 14 oz plain flour
Pinch of salt
Olive or other vegetable oil

Work together the flour and salt with a little water (yeast is omitted in this recipe). Let it rest about 30 minutes, then divide it into small balls and roll each one out to about 3 mm / $\frac{1}{8}$ in and 12–15 cm / $4\frac{1}{2}$–6 in in diameter, but they can be larger or smaller.

The filling can be made in various ways. The best known perhaps and also the easiest is a slice of Mozzarella cheese with anchovy fillet. 350 g / 12 oz of Mozzarella and 4–5 anchovies, washed and chopped, should be enough. Fold the edge over the stuffing, pinch the edges together and fry gently in plenty of hot oil.

125 FRIED PIZZA [2]

The recipe is the same, but add 15 ml / 1 tbls of blanched, peeled, seeded and chopped tomato to the Mozzarella slice or spread the tomato on top of the fried pizza.

Fried pizza [*1*]

126   FRIED PIZZA [3]

Here is another classic version with a different filling. Mix 3–4 medium-sized eggs with 225 g/8 oz Ricotta cheese, 30–45 ml/2–3 tbls peeled, cubed fresh sausage and 15 ml/1 tbls chopped parsley.

127   FRIED PIZZA [4]

Instead of the raw eggs in version [3], use boiled eggs and chopped black olives.

128 FRIED PIZZA [5]

These are more elementary than the others, yet they are very appetizing. The dough is the same as described in the others but you make circles $7\frac{1}{2}$–10 cm/3–4 in in diameter and 3 mm/$\frac{1}{8}$ in, or less, thick. Fry them in plenty of hot oil, then drain them and immediately garnish them with blanched, peeled, seeded and chopped tomatoes and fresh basil leaves. The heat of the pizza will heat the tomatoes.

Of course they can also be garnished with Mozzarella or other ingredients, but there is not the same affinity as with the tomatoes and basil.

129 SGABEI-DONZELLINE

These are made with leavened dough and no other ingredients are added to the dough. Make a dough following recipe **120**. Let the leavened dough rest for 30 minutes in a warm place covered with a cloth. Then on a pastry board, divide it into pieces and roll out each piece into the shape of a finger about 10 cm/4 in long and about 12 m/$\frac{1}{2}$ in wide. Fry these in plenty of hot oil. They will swell a little as they fry, like thick homemade breadsticks. They are extremely tasty, having rustic simplicity and are ideal as an accompaniment to prosciutto, ham and cheese. The *Sgabei* still have a place of honour in Lunigiana.

In some parts of Tuscany, little pieces of fried bread dough, similar to the *sgabei* but smaller, are charmingly called *donzelline*, meaning 'little ladies'. Sometimes a sprinkling of chopped thyme or other herbs is added to the dough.

130 SCIATT

Sciatt, which means 'toad', is a fritter made with cheese-enriched batter, and is made in Valtellina, a mountainous region in northern Italy. The dough can be made with buckwheat flour and plain flour in equal parts, or two-thirds buckwheat and one-third plain flour. Altogether you will need 400 g/14 oz flour. (Buckwheat flour is increasingly available at wholefood shops and speciality food stores.)

Mix the flour and a large pinch of salt together and add as much water as necessary to get a thick batter. Let this rest for an hour, then add a bland cheese such as Mozzarella, cut into pieces, and a small glass of grappa, marc or other fruit brandy. Mix this well so that the cheese is evenly distributed throughout the batter, then drop it by spoonfuls in plenty of hot olive oil. Let them become golden brown on both sides so the cheese melts. (Be sure you have included some cheese in each spoonful before you drop it into the oil.) Drain them well on absorbent paper and serve hot.

Sgabei-donzelline

131 PANZEROTTI [1]

These are small fried pizza made with a dough that is lighter than the usual pizza dough. For six people you will need:

    400 g / 14 oz plain flour
    Pinch of salt
    25 g / 1 oz brewer's yeast dissolved in a little water

Add the salt to the flour and gradually add the dissolved yeast. Only add more water if the dough becomes too hard. Let it rest for 30 minutes in a cool place, knead well, then divide it into small pieces. Roll out each one into a circle about 3 m / $\frac{1}{8}$ in thick. On half the circle, put a few slices of Mozzarella (300 g / 11 oz in all) and one or two pieces of rinsed and chopped anchovy. Then fold the other side over it, pinch the edges together gently and fry in oil.

You could also add a little blanched, peeled, seeded and chopped tomato to the filling instead of the anchovies or use all three, tomatoes, cheese and anchovies – always a pleasing combination in these little pizzas.

132 PANZEROTTI [2]

Follow the recipe in Panzerotti [1], but make the filling as follows: Mix 3–4 medium-sized eggs with about 300 g / 11 oz Ricotta cheese and 45 ml / 3 tbls of chopped, fresh sausage.

133 CHIZZE

These are a kind of *panzerotti* from the Emilia region. For six people you will need:

    400 g / 14 oz plain flour
    25 g / 1 oz brewer's yeast dissolved in a little tepid water
    Pinch of salt
    50 g / 2 oz lard
    Parmesan cheese, grated, or Ricotta cheese, chopped
    Olive or other vegetable oil

Mix the flour with the dissolved yeast. Work in the lard and add a pinch of salt. The dough should be smooth and firm. Add more water gradually if necessary. Let this rest for 30 minutes in a cool spot, covered with a cloth. Then roll it out to a thickness of 3 mm / $\frac{1}{8}$ in and cut it into squares approximately 10 cm / 4 in to a side. Cover half of each square with 15 ml / 1 tbls Parmesan, Ricotta or other cheese. Fold the other side over it, pinch the edges together and fry the *chizze* in plenty of oil. Drain them well on absorbent paper and serve immediately.

Panzerotti [*1*]

134   CASSONI [1]

These are another type of *panzerotti* Emilia-style. For 6 people you will need:

400 g / 14 oz plain flour   3 medium-sized eggs   45 ml / 3 tbls milk

Pinch of salt   Lard

Make a smooth, firm dough with the flour, eggs, milk and salt. Roll the dough out 3 mm / $\frac{1}{8}$ in thick and cut circles 10–12.5 cm / 4–5 in in diameter. On half of each circle spread a little of the following filling:

Clean and boil 800 g / $1\frac{3}{4}$ lb of spinach, beet spinach or other greens in water just to cover. Drain well and cut them up very finely. Mix 45–60 ml / 3–4 tbls grated Parmesan or similar cheese with them and divide this among the circles. Fold the free side over the filling and pinch the edges together. Fry in a generous amount of lard, drain on absorbent paper and serve hot.

In another version, a filling is made with onions gently sautéed in butter.

Cassoni [1]

135 CASSONI [2]

In this old-fashioned version, the filling is made with a mixture of greens, boiled and chopped as in the preceding recipe, and raisins and chopped pine nuts.

136 CALCIONI ABRUZZESI

This is a stuffed and fried dough. For six people you will need:

    400 g / 14 oz plain flour   2 medium-sized eggs   100 g / 4 oz lard
    1–2 tablespoons lemon juice   Olive or other vegetable oil

Mix the flour, eggs, lard, salt and lemon juice together to obtain a soft but firm dough. Let this rest for 30 minutes. For the filling you will need:

    300 g / 11 oz Ricotta cheese   2 medium-sized egg yolks
    100 g / 4 oz prosciutto or cooked ham, chopped
    100 g / 4 oz Provolone cheese, cut into small cubes
    10 ml / 2 tsp chopped parsley

Calcioni abruzzesi

Combine the filling ingredients. Roll out the dough into 2 thin sheets. On one of the sheets, distribute the filling at regular intervals. Cover with the second sheet. Press the unfilled space around the fillings together, then cut around them with a small cutting wheel.

Fry these *calcioni* in plenty of hot oil, then drain them well on absorbent paper before serving. In the Abruzzo they almost always accompany this with pieces of vegetables, Scamorza cheese and brains, all fried to make what is called a *fritto misto*.

137 PANZEROTTI ROMAN-STYLE

The name *panzerotti* suggests the other *panzerotti* but there is an important variation in the dough. For six people you will need:

300 g / 11 oz plain flour
    Pinch of salt
    3 medium-sized egg yolks
    50 g / 2 oz softened butter

Add the salt to the flour and mix it with the egg yolks and butter. Add enough water to make a soft elastic dough. Roll the dough out into a sheet, not too thin, and make circles 12–15 cm / $4\frac{1}{2}$–6 in in diameter. On half the circle, spread a filling made with:

    100 g / 4 oz prosciutto or cooked ham, cut into small cubes
    100 g / 4 oz Gruyère or Fontina cheese, cut into small cubes
    2 medium-sized eggs
    50 g / 2 tbls Parmesan cheese, grated
    Salt and freshly ground black pepper
    Olive or other vegetable oil

Combine these ingredients to make a soft but not too dry mixture. Spread this filling on the circles, fold the edges over and press them together.

Fry these Roman-style *panzerotti* in a pan with plenty of hot oil.

138 TIGELLE [1]

This is a dish which dates back a long way, from the days when man began to mix flour and water and simply roast it over red-hot stones. Tigelle are still made like this in the Apennines today, though in a slightly less crude way. For six people you will need:

    400 g / 14 oz plain flour
    Pinch of salt
    20 g / $\frac{3}{4}$ oz brewer's yeast dissolved in a little warm water
    50 g / 2 oz lard
    Lard

Add the salt to the flour, then work in the yeast and the lard to get a smooth well-mixed dough. Let this rise in a warm place for 1 hour, covered with a cloth, then roll out a sheet 3 m / $\frac{1}{8}$ in thick. On the sheet cut circles about 10 cm / 4 in in diameter and fry them in plenty of hot lard. Drain on absorbent paper, then slice them horizontally to form 2 circles. On one half, spread a filling made of chopped streaky bacon, about 50 g / 2 oz, garlic to taste and a few rosemary leaves. Cover with the other half and serve hot.

In the traditional method, no yeast is added and the dough is tougher and heavier. To be completely authentic, the circles are baked on clay discs, called *tigelli*, that were made just for this purpose and greased with lard. They are still found in that area. The circles of dough on the discs are filled with chestnut leaves and put on the open hearth to bake, over the coals, thus absorbing the fragrance of the chestnut leaves.

Tigelle [1]

139 TIGELLE [2]

These *tigelle* are prepared the same as in [1] but the filling consists of grated Pecorino or Romano cheese, which the heat of the hot *tigelle* should melt nicely.

140 PIADINE

Like *tigelle, piadine* come from the most ancient tradition of bread-making. The recipe comes from the flat Po River area in the Romagna region in north-eastern Italy, while the *tigelle* recipe comes from the mountains. For six people you will need:

Pinch of salt
500 g / 18 oz plain flour
150 g / 5 oz lard, softened

Add the salt to the flour and work in the lard, adding enough tepid water to get a soft but consistent dough. Divide this dough into pieces and shape them into small circles a little over 3 mm / $\frac{1}{8}$ in thick. These *piadine* are grilled, with no other oil or additives, on a heavy iron frying-pan or griddle. They were originally cooked on large clay discs called *testi*. To make them softer, prick them with a fork as they cook. *Piadine* are still used as bread in Romagna. They can also be served covered or split and filled with ham or cheese such as Mozzarella.

Another very appetizing version is to cut them in half, fill them with chopped watercress and grated or Bel Paese cheese to serve as sandwiches, hot or cold.

141 CROSTATA WITH ONIONS

The crostata is a tart which differs from the *torta rustica* (recipe **187**) in that the dough is more delicate. The preparation is also more elaborate, though at times the differences can be minimal. While a bread dough is often used for *focaccia* (recipe **156**) and the *torta rustica*, for the crostata you must use the following dough which serves six people:

300 g / 11 oz plain flour
Salt
150 g / 5 oz butter, softened

Add a pinch of salt to the flour. Work the flour mixture and butter together so the butter is as well absorbed as possible. Continue to work it together, adding water gradually as needed to get a homogeneous, smooth and elastic dough. Knead more gently than with previous doughs. Shape it into a ball and let it rest for 30 minutes in a cool place, covered with a cloth.

Meanwhile prepare a filling:

1 kg / 2$\frac{1}{4}$ lb onions, chopped
50 g / 2 oz butter
6 anchovy fillets, washed and chopped
100 ml / 4 fl oz single cream
15 ml / 1 tbls plain flour
Salt and freshly ground black pepper
1 medium-sized egg, beaten

Cook the onions gently in the butter until translucent, along with the anchovies. When the onions are ready and the anchovies have begun to disintegrate, add the cream and the flour, stirring well so the mixture thickens. Season with salt and pepper. Remove from the heat and quickly mix in the beaten egg.

When the dough has rested sufficiently, heat the oven to 220 C / 425 F / gas 7. Knead the dough again briefly, then roll it out into a round about 3 mm // $\frac{1}{8}$ in thick. Butter a 30 cm / 12 in tart tin, flour it and put the sheet of dough on it, pushing up

Crostata with onions

the sides to form a low edge. Prick just the surface of the dough with a fork. Pour the onion mixture over the dough and bake until the filling has set and the crust is golden.

If you have any left-over dough, you can make a lattice-work to cover the filling. Another idea is to boil 12 tiny onions, drain them very well, sauté them in a little butter and put them around the edge of the dough before baking.

Another method is to bake the dough separately for 20 minutes, weighing the surface down with dried beans on greaseproof paper. The dough will then be rather dry. Remove the greaseproof paper and beans, spread the filling over it and put it back in the oven for about ten minutes.

142   CROSTATA WITH LEEKS

For six people you will need:
  Dough recipe **141**
  900 g / 2 lb leeks, cleaned very well
  30 ml / 2 tbls olive oil
  25 g / 1 oz butter
  Salt and freshly ground black pepper
  3 medium-sized eggs, beaten
  75 g / 3 fl oz single cream
  45 ml / 3 tbls grated Parmesan cheese

Heat the oven to 220 C / 425 F / gas 7 and roll out the dough. Cut the white part into thin slices and save the rest for another dish. Melt the oil and butter over a low heat, add the leeks and sauté them gently so they do not brown. Season with salt and pepper, remove from the heat and add the eggs, cream and cheese. Mix well and pour over the dough and bake.

Crostata with leeks

143 CROSTATA WITH GREEN PEPPERS

For six people you will need:

    Dough recipe **141**

    4–5 large green peppers, seeded and cut into strips

    90 ml / 6 tbls olive oil

    6 medium-sized tomatoes, blanched, peeled, seeded and chopped

    1 large onion, sliced

    Heat the oven to 220 C / 425 F / gas 7 and roll out the dough. The peppers can be roasted under a grill and then peeled, if wished. Heat the oil in a pan over medium heat and add the other ingredients. Let them cook, stirring occasionally, until they have become soft. Pour the mixture over the dough and bake.

Crostata with green peppers

Crostata with carrots

144 CROSTATA WITH CARROTS

For six people you will need:

    Dough recipe **141**   900 g / 2 lb carrots, peeled, boiled and sliced

    50 g / 2 oz butter   125 ml / 4 fl oz beef or chicken stock

    100 g / 4 oz Mozzarella cheese, cut in thin slices

    30 ml / 2 tbls grated Parmesan cheese

Heat the oven to 220 C / 425 F / gas 7 and roll out the dough. Sauté the boiled carrots in the butter, adding stock as necessary to keep a little liquid at the bottom of the pan. Let this reduce to thicken a little and add salt and pepper. Reserve one quarter of the mixture and purée through a sieve or in a blender. Pour the purée over the dough. Place the slices of Mozzarella over the purée, then garnish with the reserved carrots. Sprinkle the Parmesan over this, dot with butter and bake.

145 CROSTATA WITH COURGETTES

For six people you will need:

    Dough recipe **141**   1 large onion, chopped   30 ml / 2 tbls olive oil

    25 g / 1 oz butter   900 g / 2 lb medium-sliced courgettes, sliced

    4 medium-sized tomatoes, peeled, seeded and crushed (optional)

    Salt and freshly ground black pepper   2 medium-sized eggs, beaten

    30 ml / 2 tbls grated Parmesan cheese

Heat the oven to 220 C / 425 F / gas 7 and roll out the dough. Sauté the onion in the butter and oil, then add the courgettes. Let them brown a little, then add the tomatoes, if wished, salt and pepper. Cook briefly, remove from the heat and immediately stir in the eggs and cheese. Pour the filling over the dough and bake.

Crostata with courgettes

146   CROSTATA WITH ARTICHOKES AND CHEESE

For six people you will need:
  Dough recipe **141**
  12 large artichokes
  15 ml / 1 tbls lemon juice
  50 g / 2 oz butter
  Salt and freshly ground black pepper
  25 g / 1 oz chopped parsley
  175 g / 6 oz Fontina, Gruyère or
    Taleggio cheese or a mixture of
    them, cubed
  45 ml / 3 tbls Parmesan cheese
  175 g / 6 fl oz single cream

Remove the artichokes' leaves and chokes. Cut the hearts into thin slices and put them in water to cover with the lemon juice so they do not turn colour. Heat the oven to 220 C / 425 F / gas 7 and roll out the dough. Drain the artichoke hearts well, then brown them in the butter, adding salt, pepper and parsley. Spread this over the dough and on top with the cubed cheese. Finally sprinkle over the Parmesan, then the cream and bake.

147 MOZZARELLA IN CARROZZA

This is a very delicious combination of bread and Mozzarella cheese. It should be eaten as soon as it is fried, while it is still hot. Unfortunately it is often made ahead in pizzerias and allowed to cool. This diminishes its appeal. For six people you will need:

24 slices of white bread, with slices about 1 cm / $\frac{3}{8}$ in thick

12 similar-sized slices of Mozzarella cheese, about 2 cm / $\frac{3}{4}$ in thick

About 5 medium-sized eggs, beaten

Flour

About 50 ml / 2 fl oz milk

Large pinch of salt

Olive oil

Freshly ground black pepper

Put each slice of cheese between 2 slices of bread. Lightly coat each sandwich with flour, then coat it on all sides in the eggs mixed with the milk and salt. Let the sandwiches soak in this liquid for an hour, turning them once or twice. Then heat a generous amount of olive oil in a frying-pan and fry the sandwiches until they are golden brown on both sides, turning once. Drain them well, grind a little pepper over them and serve immediately.

Mozzarella in carrozza

148   CROSTATA WITH MUSHROOMS [1]

Dough recipe **141**   300 g / 11 oz mushrooms, cleaned and sliced
175 g / 3 oz butter   Salt and freshly ground black pepper
125 ml / 4 fl oz dry white wine or dry Marsala
75 ml / 3 fl oz single cream   25 g / 1 oz parsley, chopped

Heat the oven to 220 C / 425 F / gas 7 and roll out the dough. Sauté the mushrooms in the butter. Add salt, pepper and the wine and continue to cook 1 minute. Add the cream and parsley, stir to blend and remove from the heat. Pour this over the dough and bake. Another version adds béchamel sauce instead of cream.

149   CROSTATA WITH MUSHROOMS [2]

Dough recipe **141**   300 g / 11 oz mushrooms, cleaned and sliced
75 g / 3 oz butter   300 g / 11 oz Ricotta cheese
3 medium-sized eggs, separated   45 ml / 3 tbls grated Parmesan cheese

Heat the oven to 220 C / 425 F / gas 7 and roll out the dough. Sauté the mushrooms in the butter and set them aside to cool. Mix the Ricotta with the egg yolks and Parmesan and add salt and pepper to taste. Blend this into the mushrooms. Beat the whites till stiff but not dry. Gently fold them into the mushroom-cheese mixture. Pour this over the dough and bake.

In a still richer version, you can add 100 g / 4 oz diced prociutto or cooked ham to the mushrooms.

150   CROSTATA WITH CHEESE

Dough recipe **141**   275 g / 10 oz Fontina, Gruyère or Taleggio cheese
3 medium-sized eggs, beaten   45 ml / 3 tbls Parmesan cheese, grated
100 ml / 4 fl oz white wine   Pinch of freshly ground nutmeg
Salt and freshly ground black pepper

Heat the oven to 220 C / 425 F / gas 7 and roll out the dough. Cut the cheese into thin strips and cover the dough with them. Mix the eggs with the Parmesan and the wine, adding the nutmeg and salt and pepper to taste. Pour this over the dough and bake.

151   CROSTATA WITH HAM

Dough recipe **141**   250 g / 9 oz prosciutto or cooked ham, diced
4 medium-sized eggs, beaten   175 ml / 6 fl oz single cream
Pinch of freshly ground nutmeg   Salt and freshly ground black pepper

Heat the oven to 220 C / 425 F / gas 7 and roll out the dough. Beat the eggs with the cream, add the nutmeg, salt and pepper to taste and the diced prosciutto or ham. Pour this over the dough and bake.

152   CROSTATA WITH PANCETTA

Pancetta is a kind of rolled very fatty ham. You can substitute streaky bacon for pancetta. For six people you will need:

Dough recipe **141**   3 medium-sized eggs   75 ml / 3 fl oz single cream
Salt and freshly ground black pepper
200 g / 7 oz Gruyère or Fontina cheese, cut into thin slices
200 g / 7 oz pancetta or streaky bacon, cut into very thin slices

Heat the oven to 220/425 F/gas 7 and roll out the dough. Beat the eggs with the cream, adding salt and pepper to taste. Spread alternating layers of cheese and pancetta over the dough, cover with the egg-cream mixture and bake.

153   CROSTATA WITH RICOTTA AND SAUSAGE

Dough recipe **141**   250 g/9 oz Ricotta cheese   3 medium-sized egg yolks
100 g/4 oz fresh sausage, crumbled or finely chopped
45 ml/3 tbls grated Parmesan cheese   Salt and freshly ground black pepper
Pinch of freshly ground nutmeg

Heat the oven to 220 C/425 F/gas 7 and roll out the dough. Mix the Ricotta with the egg yolks, sausage, and the Parmesan. Season with salt and pepper and the nutmeg. Blend this together, pour it onto the dough and bake.

154   BORLENGHI

This recipe is one of the oldest dishes coming from the Emilian region between Modena and its border with Tuscany.

Make a batter by adding water to 400 g/14 oz plain flour, little by little, until it is fluid and not too thick. Add a pinch of salt. Heat the biggest and heaviest frying-pan until it is very hot. Grease it lightly with lard and pour in a big spoonful of the batter so that it covers the bottom of the pan, forming a very thin pancake. It will

Crostata with Ricotta and sausage

cook in an instant. Cook the borlenghi one by one. They are best drained on absorbent paper and served immediately. As they cook, you can spread over 15 ml/1 tbls of a seasoning made by mashing together chopped bacon fat, chopped garlic and rosemary.

155 TESTAROI-PANICACCI

At the top of the hills of Lerici, beneath a castle built before 1,000 A.D. is the little region of Trebiano, still intact with some medieval houses and narrow streets. At the foot of the castle is the Locanda delle Sette Lune, an inn or *trattoria* where the cook makes old fashioned dishes like *testaroi* or *testaroli*, a name coming from the Latin word *testum*, meaning 'earthen pot'. *Testaroi* are fried or grilled dough and are one of the oldest doughs in the world. They originated when early versions of schiacciata, bread and pizza were really the same, just used in different ways.

Lucia makes her dough with 'spelt' flour, made from an ancient grain that is still collected wild in this region of Lunigiana, though each year there is less. For 6 people, 500 g/18 oz plain flour, water and salt are used, nothing else.

Mix the dough and salt with enough water to get a rather thin batter. Now heat a pan, preferably cast iron, which will substitute for the old-fashioned earthenware pots once used. Do not grease the pan, or you can wipe it with the cut side of potato and grease lightly. When the pan is hot, pour a little batter over it, tipping it to form a circle that will cook quickly without sticking or turning over.

The testaroi are seasoned with the classic Ligurian pesto, made with basil, oil,

Testaroi-panicacci

Pecorino cheese and *prescinseua,* a kind of farmer's cheese, along with a few pine nuts. Or it is simply seasoned with oil and grated Pecorino. I consider them a kind of *schiacciata* or *pizzetta.* These are quite separate from other *testaroi* which are larger and cut into strips, then thrown into a pot of vegetables just like the ancient Roman *laganum,* the ancestor of thin noodles (*tagliatelle*).

Other versions of testaroi are made smaller and the batter is thicker.

156   FOCACCIA

Focaccia is like a very thick pizza with a more bread-like texture. It is usually seasoned lightly and eaten as a snack. This, like the other recipes, serves six.

> 400 g / 14 oz preferably strong white flour, or plain flour
> Pinch of salt
> 25 g / 1 oz fresh yeast or 12 g / $\frac{1}{2}$ oz dried active baking yeast, dissolved in a little water

Mix a pinch of salt with the flour and add the dissolved yeast and enough water to make a soft but firm dough. Knead till smooth and elastic. Let this rise at least 1 hour, then roll it out and put it in a round greased 25 cm / 10 in flan tin. It should be about 4 cm / 1$\frac{1}{2}$ in thick. Heat the oven to 200 C / 400 F / gas 6 and when hot, bake the focaccia for an hour. Let it cool before cutting and serving. It is very good with cheese, prosciutto, ham, salami and so on.

You can make a softer and more flavourful focaccia by mixing 50 g / 2 oz of the flour with the yeast and water and letting this rise for 30 minutes in a warm, draught-free place, covered with a cloth. Then knead in the remaining flour, adding 30–45 ml / 2–3 tbls melted lard or olive oil. You can also add a few leaves of rosemary or sage, finely chopped, to the dough as you knead it.

Focaccia

157 FOCACCIA WITH TOMATO AND GARLIC

This version of *focaccia* is characteristic of Puglia in southern Italy where it is called *puddica*. The dough is the same as that described above in the simpler version. Roll it out in the *focaccia* shape in a flan tin greased with oil and then poke little indentations on the surface with your finger and put little pieces of garlic and blanched, peeled and seeded tomatoes in them. Sprinkle with salt and oregano, moisten with oil and bake in a 200 C/400 F/gas 6 oven for 30–40 minutes.

158 PIZZA RUSTICA [1]

Although this is called a pizza, it is actually a *focaccia*.

> Pinch of salt
> 400 g/14 oz preferably strong white flour, or plain flour
> 60 ml/4 tbls olive oil
> White wine or water

Add a pinch of salt to the flour and combine the oil and flour. Add white wine (which is the old-fashioned Puglian way) or water, little by little, till you get a soft dough. Knead till smooth and elastic. There is no yeast. Now prepare this filling.

> 200 g/7 oz Ricotta cheese
> 200 g/7 oz Mozzarella cheese, cubed
> 100 g/4 oz Bel Paese or similar cheese, cubed
> 100 g/4 oz sausage, preferably a spicy one, cut into small pieces
> 3–4 medium-sized eggs, beaten, plus extra for brushing

Heat the oven to 200 C/400 F/gas 6. Mix together the Ricotta, Mozzarella, the soft cheese, sausage and eggs and reserve. Roll the dough out into 2 round 25 cm/10 in sheets about 3 mm/$\frac{1}{8}$ in thick, one a little larger than the other. The larger one should fit into a greased 25 cm/10 in pie plate but be big enough to go up the sides of the pan a little to form a rim. Spread the filling on it, then cover with the second sheet and pinch the edges together. Brush with a little beaten egg and bake for 45 minutes.

You can also cover the top with a lattice-work made from the dough instead of the second sheet.

159 PIZZA RUSTICA [2]

Replace the sausage with chopped prosciutto or cooked ham sautéed briefly in a little olive oil.

Focaccia with tomatoes and garlic

160 FOCACCIA WITH ONIONS, UMBRIAN-STYLE

350 g/12 oz preferably strong white flour, or plain flour
25 g/1 oz fresh yeast, or 12 g/½ oz dried active baking yeast, dissolved in a little
  lukewarm water   75 g/3 oz lard, softened
60 ml/4 tbls olive oil   Pinch of salt   150 g/1 lb onions, thinly sliced
About 60 ml/4 tbls fresh sage, finely chopped

Make a starter dough with 50 g/2 oz of the flour and the dissolved yeast, adding more water till the dough is firm but workable. Let this rise in a warm, draught-free place, covered with a cloth, for an hour. Then work in the rest of the flour, again adding water, little by little, as needed. Knead until smooth and elastic. Shape it into a ball, make a cut on top in the shape of a cross and put it in a warm, draught-free place to rise, covered with a cloth, for two hours. Knead it a third time, working in the lard, the oil and salt. Grease a round 20 cm/8 in flan tin and spread the dough over the bottom. Scatter the sliced onions over the dough, sprinkle the sage over

Focaccia with onions, Umbrian-style

the onions, moisten with oil and let this rise at least 30 minutes. Bake in a 200 C / 400 F / gas 6 oven until golden brown.

161 FOCACCIA LIGURIAN-STYLE WITH ONIONS

For six people you will need:

400 g / 14 oz preferably strong white flour, or plain flour

25 g / 1 oz fresh yeast or 12 g / ½ oz dried active baking yeast, dissolved in a little warm water   Pinch of salt   Olive oil

1 medium-sized onion, sliced   Salt

Mix the flour with salt and work in the dissolved yeast. Add enough water, little by little, to make a soft but firm dough. Knead well. Let it rise in a cool spot for 30 minutes, covered with a cloth. Heat the oven to 200 C / 400 F / gas 6. Roll the dough out to a thickness of 4 cm / 1½ in and place it on a greased round 25 cm / 10 in flan tin.

Focaccia Ligurian-style with onions

Poke little indentations on the surface with your finger and dribble olive oil over this, then scatter the sliced onion over the top, sprinkle with salt and bake until golden brown.

162 SFINCIUNI

A country dish from Palermo, it is a bit complicated but enchanting. For six people you will need:

90 ml/6 tbls olive oil   Juice of one lemon

.Salt and freshly ground black pepper

60 ml/4 tbls Pecorino, Romano or Caciocavallo cheese, grated

400 g/14 oz preferably strong white flour, or plain flour

25 g/1 oz fresh yeast or 12 g/½ oz dried active baking yeast, dissolved in a little water

Heat the olive oil and add the lemon juice, salt, pepper and the cheese. Work this mixture into the flour, then add the dissolved yeast. You should get a soft but firm dough. Knead well. Put it into a bowl dusted with a little flour, make a cross-shaped cut in the top and let it rise for 2 hours, covered with a cloth, in a warm draught-free place.

For the topping you will need:

150 ml/5 fl oz olive oil   One large onion

500 g/18 lb tomatoes, blanched, peeled, seeded and chopped

30 ml/2 tbls chopped parsley

100 g/4 oz Pecorino, Romano or Cacciocavallo cheese, cut into small pieces

6 anchovy fillets, washed, dried and chopped

30 ml/2 tbls dry bread crumbs

While the dough rises, prepare the topping. Heat 75 ml/3 fl oz of the oil in a pan and add the onions and the tomatoes. Let them cook for a few minutes to bind them, then add the parsley, the cheese and two-thirds of the anchovies. Cook gently over a low heat for 10–15 minutes. Reserve.

When the dough is ready, briefly knead it again and spread it on a round greased 25 cm/10 in flan tin. Let it rise for another 30 minutes in a warm, draught-free place. Heat the oven to 200 C/400 F/gas 6. When the dough is ready, poke indentations into the top with your finger and spread half the sauce over it. Bake for 30 minutes.

Meanwhile, heat the rest of the oil in a frying-pan with the bread crumbs. Take the *sfinciuni* out of the oven and cover it with the rest of the sauce, garnish it with the rest of the anchovies and sprinkle over the bread crumbs. Moisten with a little more olive oil and bake another 10 minutes and serve.

163 FOCACCIA (GNOCCO) WITH CRACKLINGS [1]

Ciccioli are the cracklings which remain after you melt the pork fat to get lard. A good substitute is finely crumbled cooked bacon. For six people you will need:

600 g/21 oz preferably strong white flour, or plain flour

25 g/1 oz brewer's yeast dissolved in a little warm water

175 g/6 oz lard, softened

225 g/8 oz cracklings or finely crumbled cooked bacon

Work the flour, dissolved yeast and lard together on a pastry board. Reserve a handful of the cracklings or bacon and add the rest to the dough. Knead until it is very smooth and soft and the cracklings or bacon are well distributed. Spread it in a greased and floured 30 cm/12 in round flan tin. Sprinkle the reserved cracklings over the dough, pressing them gently in. Let it rise about 1 hour in a warm, draught-free place, then put it in a 200 C/400 F/gas 6 oven. It is ready when it has puffed up and become golden on top. It is delicious hot or cold.

Focaccia (gnocco) with cracklings [1]

164 FOCACCIA WITH CRACKLINGS [2]

This is the Calabrian version, especially from Ardore. For six people you will need:

500 g / 18 oz preferably strong white flour, or plain flour

Pinch of salt

25 g / 1 oz fresh yeast or 12 g / $\frac{1}{2}$ oz dried active baking yeast, dissolved in a little water

60 ml / $2\frac{1}{2}$ fl oz olive oil

3 medium-sized eggs

Add the salt to the flour and mix it with the dissolved yeast, adding more water, little by little, to get a soft but firm dough. Knead well. Let it rise for an hour, covered with a cloth, in a cool place. Work the olive oil and eggs into the dough, kneading it until smooth and pliable. Then divide it into two pieces, one slightly larger than the other and roll them into two round sheets about 12 mm / $\frac{1}{2}$ in thick. Line a round greased and floured 20 cm / 8 in flan tin with the larger sheet of dough.

Sardenaira

For the filling:
>   100 g / 4 oz Ricotta cheese   3 hard-boiled eggs, shelled and sliced
>   175 g / 6 oz cracklings or finely crumbled cooked bacon
>   100 g / 4 oz prosciutto or cooked ham, thinly sliced and diced
>   100 g / 4 oz Mozzarella or Provolone cheese, sliced

Mix the filling ingredients together and spread them over the larger sheet of dough. Cover with the top sheet, pinch the edges together and set it aside to rise for another hour. Bake in a 200 C / 400 F / gas 6 oven for 30 minutes or until golden brown. Check occasionally and lower the heat if it is browning too fast.

165   TORTANO WITH CRACKLINGS

In Naples *ciccioli* are called *cicoli* and there is a pizza or tart made with them called *tortano*, a very special dish. For six people you will need:
>   500 g / 18 oz preferably strong white flour, or plain flour
>   25 g / 1 oz brewer's yeast dissolved in a little water
>   Salt and coarsely ground black pepper   25 g / 4 oz lard
>   100 g / 4 oz cracklings or finely crumbled cooked bacon

Make a starter dough with 50 g / 2 oz flour, the dissolved yeast, salt and a good sprinkling of fragrant pepper. Let this rise in a cool place under a cloth for 1 hour. Pour the rest of the flour onto a pastry board, make a well in the centre and put the starter dough inside. Gradually work it together, adding the lard and the cracklings or bacon. Knead this and then let it rise in a cool spot for 30 minutes. Briefly knead again, and spread onto a round greased 25 cm / 10 in flan tin, and bake in a 200 C / 400 F / gas 6 oven until it is golden.

The classic version of this 'pizza' uses a round baking tin with high sides and a hole in the middle as is used for angel food cakes.

166   SARDENAIRA

Although this is called a Sardenaira pizza, it is really a *focaccia*. In Liguria, where it is from, it is also called a *pizzalandrea* which is a simplification of 'pizza all'Andrea', from the name of a famous admiral, Andrea Doria, who supposedly invented it (though probably he liked it so much it was named after him). For six people you will need:
>   425 g / 15 oz preferably strong white flour, or plain flour
>   25 g / 1 oz brewer's yeast dissolved in a little warm water
>   50 ml / 4 tbls olive oil   Pinch of salt   Milk (optional)

Make a mound with the flour and in the centre pour in the dissolved yeast. Begin to work it together, adding the oil and the salt. If you find the dough becoming too hard or not elastic enough, mix a little milk with some water and add this, a little at a time, until you have a soft, firm but elastic dough. Knead well. Let this rise in a cool spot, covered with a cloth, for 2 hours. Meanwhile prepare the following filling.
>   300 g / 11 oz onions, sliced
>   60 ml / 4 tbls olive oil
>   3 medium-sized tomatoes, blanched, peeled, seeded and coarsely chopped
>   Fresh basil leaves, wiped clean
>   4–6 achovy fillets, washed and chopped   1–2 garlic cloves, sliced
>   Black olives

Sauté the onions in the oil without letting them brown, then add the tomatoes, stirring occasionally. Add the basil leaves and anchovies and cook briefly. When the dough is ready, knead it again briefly, then roll it out onto a round greased and floured 25 cm / 10 in flan tin so that the edges of the dough extend up the sides about 12 mm /

$\frac{1}{2}$ in high. Spread the onion mixture over the dough, garnish with a few slices of garlic and a few black olive halves. Bake in a 200 C/400 F/gas 6 oven for about 30 minutes or until golden.

167 PIZZA RUSTICA, UMBRIAN-STYLE

For six people you will need:

    500 g / 18 oz preferably strong white flour, or plain flour
    25 g / 1 oz fresh yeast or 12 g / $\frac{1}{2}$ oz dried active baking yeast, dissolved in a little
      warm water
    4 medium-sized eggs plus 2 yolks
    125 g / 4 oz Pecorino or Romano cheese, cubed or coarsely grated
    125 g / 4 oz Parmesan cheese, grated
    About 125 ml / 4 fl oz olive oil

Make a starter dough with 225 g / 8 oz of the flour and the dissolved yeast, adding more water, little by little, till you have a soft but firm dough. Let this rise in a warm, draught-free place, under a cloth, for 1 hour. Add the rest of the flour and enough water to make a smooth, elastic but firm dough. Knead well and spread over the pastry board. Now mix the eggs, egg yolks, Pecorino and Parmesan together and work them all into the dough, adding olive oil, little by little, to make a soft but firm dough. (You may not use all the oil or you may need a little more.)

Let this dough rise for 2 hours, covered with a cloth, in a warm, draught-free place. Roll it into a round and put it on a greased round 25 cm / 10 in flan tin with high sides. Let it rise again for 1 hour in a warm spot. Bake in a 200 C/400 F/gas 6 oven until it is nicely browned.

This pizza is excellent eaten as it comes out of the oven or it can be quickly garnished with black truffles or slices of hard-boiled eggs and salami.

168 FOCACCIA JESI-STYLE

This is a traditional dish from the Marche region in central Italy. It serves six.

    360 g / 12$\frac{1}{2}$ oz preferably strong white flour, or plain flour
    25 g / 1 oz brewer's yeast, dissolved in a little water
    Pinch of salt
    30 ml / 2 tbls olive oil
    3 medium-sized eggs
    100 g / 4 oz Parmesan cheese, grated
    50 g / 2 oz Pecorino or Romano cheese, grated
    50 g / 2 oz Provolone cheese, cubed

Blend 60 g / 2$\frac{1}{2}$ oz flour with the dissolved yeast, the salt and enough water, added little by little, to make a smooth, soft dough. Shape it into a ball and let it rise for about 1 hour in a warm, draught-free place, covered with a cloth.

Meanwhile, blend the rest of the flour with the oil and enough water to make another smooth soft dough. Work the eggs, Parmesan, Pecorino or Romano cheeses into the dough. Now work the two doughs together, kneading so they blend well, then place it on a greased, round 25 cm / 10 in flan tin with sides at least 25 mm / 1 in high. Bake in a 200 C/400 F/gas 6 oven till golden.

Pizza rustica, Umbrian-style

169   FOCACCIA WITH CHEESE, RECCO-STYLE

This Ligurian *focaccia* from Recco is famous, whether it comes from Gianni Carbone of the Manuelina restaurant or from Gianni and Vittoria Bisso of the U Vittoria restaurant. For six people you will need:

  600 g / 21 oz flour
  Pinch of salt
  600 g / 21 oz Stracchino or Bel Paese cheese
  Olive oil

  Blend the flour with a pinch of salt and enough water to make a smooth dough. Knead well. Let this rest in a cool spot, under a cloth, for 20 minutes. Then divide it in 2 parts and roll out 2 round sheets, one a little larger than the other, as thinly as possible, using your hands where necessary. Grease a 30 cm / 12 in flan tin with oil and put in the larger sheet which should extend a little up the sides. Spread the cheese over it and then place the second sheet on top. Press the edges together, moisten with oil and put in a 230 C / 450 F / gas 8 oven for a few minutes, until the cheese melts and the dough is golden brown.

170   FOCACCIA STUFFED WITH CHEESE

There are other versions of the *focaccia* from Recco apart from the previous classic one with cheese and they are all very tasty. For example, you can make a filling by combining Mascarpone or cream cheese mixed with a little single cream to soften it, and Gorgonzola cheese. In this case have the bottom sheet of dough a little thicker because this is a more substantial filling. The top sheet remains as thin as possible. Bake as before.

171   FOCACCIA WITH CHEESE AND PROSCIUTTO OR HAM

As with recipe **170**, the bottom sheet of dough is a little thicker and a filling is made of slices of soft cheese like Bel Paese with, thin strips of prosciutto or cooked ham.

172   FOCACCIA WITH RICOTTA AND SAUSAGE

This is similar to recipe **169**. The stuffing is made of 250 g / 9 oz of Ricotta, broken, and 250 g / 9 oz of fresh sausage, cut in small cubes.

173   FOCACCIA WITH GREENS

This time the filling is made with spinach, beet spinach, curly endive or whatever greens you prefer. You will need 3.4 kg / 3 lb greens, trimmed, boiled, drained very well, chopped and sautéed briefly in 25 g / 1 oz of butter. Add salt and pepper to taste. You can add Ricotta, sausage or ham to this, even raisins, revived in a little water, and pine nuts. The rest is the same as recipe **169**.

Focaccia with cheese, Recco-style

Focaccia with batavia

174 FOCACCIA WITH BATAVIA

Batavia has a very 'green' taste and is used cooked as well as raw in salads. For this rustic tart, popularly called a pizza, you will need for six people:

400 g / 14 oz preferably strong white flour, or plain flour

Pinch of salt

25 g / 1 oz fresh yeast or 12 g / ½ oz dried active baking yeast, dissolved in a little warm water

Make a dough by working together the flour, salt and dissolved yeast, adding more water, little by little, until the dough is soft but firm. Knead well. Let it rest in a cool spot, under a cloth, for 1 hour. Meanwhile make the filling. You will need:

6 heads of batavia, washed, par-boiled, squeezed dry and cut into strips

60 ml / 4 tbls olive oil

6 anchovy fillets, washed and chopped

175 g / 6 oz black olives, stoned and pitted

30 ml / 2 tbls capers chopped

45 ml / 3 tbls raisins, revived in warm water and drained (optional)

45 ml / 3 tbls pine nuts (optional)

Heat the olive oil in a frying-pan over medium heat with the anchovies. Add the olives, capers and finally batavia and cook 10–12 minutes so that all blends well. Then, if you want to make it the traditional way, add the raisins and pine nuts.

Roll the dough out into two round sheets, one a little larger than the other. The larger one should be about 3 mm / ⅛ in thick and it will line a greased, round 20 cm / 8 in flan tin extending up the sides a little. Spread the filling over this, then cover with the other sheet and roll and press the edges together to form a cord-like rim. Bake in a 200 C / 40 F / gas 6 oven until the crust is golden.

In a more refined version, you can use a starter dough consisting of 50 g / 2 oz of the flour and the dissolved yeast and the salt, let this rest for 1 hour, then incorporate the rest of the flour and continue as described above.

175 FOCACCIA WITH BATAVIA AND SALT COD

This recipe is the same except for the presence of salt cod. You will need:

Dough recipe **174**

700 g / 1½ lb salt cod, soaked 48 hours in cold water, changing the water 4 times, then boiled in fresh water until tender and boned

60 ml / 4 tbls olive oil

2 garlic cloves, sliced

45 ml / 3 tbls black olives, stoned and chopped

45 ml / 3 tblr capers, chopped

25 ml / 1½ tbls parsley

6 heads batavia, prepared as in recipe **174**

Heat the oven to 200 C / 400 F / gas 6 and roll out the dough. Flake the cod, then sauté it briefly in the oil with the cloves, olives, capers, and parsley. Do not use any salt. Spread half the batavia, well drained, over the bottom sheet, then pour the salt cod mixture over it. Top with the rest of the batavia, cover with the top sheet, roll and press the edges to seal and bake.

176　PIZZA WITH ONIONS, PUGLIA-STYLE

Here the word 'pizza' is used in its local context to indicate a kind of filled *focaccia* which is actually a sort of *torta rustica*. It is also called a *calzone*, but the Puglian *calzone* is really a variation of this recipe. The stuffing is pit on one half of the dough and the other side put on top forming a jewel case of flavours. To make this for six people you will need:

    400 g / 14 oz preferably strong white flour, or plain flour

    Pinch of salt

    20 g / $\frac{3}{4}$ oz brewer's yeast dissolved in a little warm water

    45–60 ml / 3–4 tbls olive oil

Make a dough by working together the flour and salt, the dissolved yeast and the oil to get a smooth soft dough. Knead well. Let it rest about 1 hour, covered with a cloth, in a cool spot.

Meanwhile prepare the filling. You will need:

    500 g / 18 oz onions, sliced and marinating in olive oil for at least 3 hours

    250 g / 9 oz tomatoes, blanched, peeled, seeded and crushed

    100 g / 4 oz black olives, stoned and chopped

    45 ml / 3 tbls capers, chopped

    3–6 anchovy fillets, washed and chopped

    25 ml / 1$\frac{1}{2}$ tbls chopped parsley

    50 g / 2 oz Pecorino or Romano cheese, grated

Drain the onions, then mix them with the tomatoes, olives, capers, anchovies, parsley and cheese. When the dough has risen, divide it into two unequal pieces. Roll them out into two sheets, 3 mm / $\frac{1}{8}$ in thick, one a bit larger than the other. Line an oiled round 20 cm / 8 in flan tin with the larger so that the edges extend up the side a little, spread the filling over it and cover with the second sheet. Roll and press the edges together into a rope-like rim. Moisten the top with oil and cook in a 200 C / 400 F gas 6 oven until golden brown.

If you want to save time you can prepare the filling by sautéing raw, sliced onions in a few tablespoons of olive oil, gradually adding the other ingredients to them. When they have cooked a little, spread them over the dough.

177　PIZZA WITH ONIONS AND CHICORY

This is a very pleasing version of the Puglian pizza with onions. The filling is made as in recipe **176**, but instead of adding cheese and tomatoes to the onions, you add 300 g / 11 oz of chicory. If the onions have been marinating in oil, the chicory should be boiled, drained and finely chopped before adding it to the other ingredients. However, if the onions are to be cooked, simply par-boil the chicory, drain well, and chop it before adding it to the frying-pan with the other ingredients.

178　PIZZA WITH ONIONS AND SALT COD

This is still another version of the Puglian pizza with onions as described above. In this case, eliminate the anchovies and add 200 g / 7 oz salt cod, soaked 48 hours in 4 changes of water, drained, boiled until tender, boned and cut into pieces.

Proceed as in recipe **176**, spreading the filling over the bottom sheet and cover with the top sheet. Moisten with oil and bake in a 200 C / 40 F / gas 6 oven until the crust is golden brown.

Pizza with onions, Puglia-style

179 PIZZA CALABRIAN-STYLE

This is still another version of *torta rustica* with onions, similar to the Puglian pizza with onions, but with its own distinct identity. For six people you will need:

    400 g / 14 oz preferably strong white flour, or plain flour
    Pinch of salt
    25 g / 1 oz fresh yeast or 12 g / ½ oz dried active baking yeast, dissolved in a little
        lukewarm water
    75 g / 3 oz lard
    1–2 medium-sized egg yolks

Make a dough with the flour, salt, the dissolved yeast, lard and the egg yolks. Knead well. Let this rest 30 minutes in a cool place, covered with a damp cloth while you prepare the filling. You need:

    90 ml / 6 tbls olive oil
    3 garlic cloves, crushed but left whole
    3 anchovy fillets, washed and chopped
    250 g / 9 oz tomatoes, blanched, peeled, seeded and sliced
    100 g / 4 oz black olives, stoned and chopped
    150 g / 5 oz canned tuna, drained

Heat the oil and brown the garlic, then discard. Gradually add the other ingredients and when they have blended together, spread over the dough prepared and bake as in recipe **176**.

180 FOCACCIA CAMPOFRANCO-STYLE

For six people you will need:

    400 g / 14 oz preferably strong white flour, or plain flour
    25 g / 1 oz fresh yeast or 12 g / ½ oz dried active baking yeast, dissolved in a little
        lukewarm water
    3 medium-sized eggs
    150 g / 5 oz butter
    Pinch of salt
    175 g / 6 oz Mozzarella cheese, sliced
    4 medium-sized tomatoes, blanched, peeled, seeded and chopped
    60 ml / 3 tbls grated Parmesan cheese

Make a starter dough with 50 g / 2 oz flour mixed with the dissolved yeast forming a very soft dough. Let this rise for an hour covered with a cloth in a cool place. Then make a mound with the rest of the dough and make a well in the centre. Put the risen dough in it and work it together, gradually incorporating the eggs and butter, adding the salt and enough water, added little by little, to make a soft but firm dough. Knead well. Spread it in a greased round 25 cm / 10 in flan tin, then let it rise for 30 minutes.

Now, put it in a cold oven and turn it on to 150 C / 300 F / gas 2 for about 40 minutes or until the dough is well cooked both inside and out but not browned. Remove the pan from the oven and turn the heat to 230 C / 450 F / gas 8. Cut in half horizontally. This will give you two large circles. Cover the lower one with three quarters of the sliced Mozzarella, then sprinkle over three quarters of the tomatoes and Parmesan cheese. Cover with the top half and spread on the rest of the Mozzarella, tomatoes and Parmesan. Bake at 230 C / 450 F / gas 8 for another 15 minutes so all ingredients get hot and well blended. Serve immediately.

In a more old-fashioned version, a few tablespoons of sugar are added to the dough.

Focaccia Campofranco-style

181 FILLED TORTANO

This is still within the most traditional dishes of Neopolitan cooking. For the *tortano*, a kind of *focaccia*, for six people, you will need:

    300 g / 1 oz preferably strong white flour, or plain flour   Salt
    25 g / 1 oz fresh yeast or 12 g / ½ oz dried active baking yeast, dissolved in a little
        lukewarm water   100 g / 4 oz lard
    45 ml / 3 tbls grated Parmesan cheese   Freshly ground black pepper

Make a starter dough by blending 50 g / 2 oz flour with the dissolved yeast and a pinch of salt. Let this rise for about 1 hour under a cloth in a warm, draught-free place, then pour the rest of the flour on a pastry board and gradually work in the risen dough, the lard, Parmesan, a little salt and a generous grinding of pepper. Add water, little by little, to get a soft dough. Knead well. Let it rise for 2 hours in a warm, draught-free spot, covered with a cloth. Meanwhile prepare the following filling:

    200 g / 7 oz Fontina, Provolone and Bel Paese cheeses, or similar cheeses,
        grated and mixed   100 g / 4 oz spicy sausage like chorizo or salami, diced
    3 medium-sized hard-boiled eggs, sliced   Softened lard, for spreading

Mix the cheeses and sausage or salami. When the dough has risen, roll it out into a round of a thickness of about 10 mm / ⅓ in, put it on a baking sheet and spread the filling on it, leaving a border of about 1 cm / ⅓ in around the edge. Be sure the dough is not too thin or the filling will break through. Over the stuffing spread the eggs. Now carefully roll the dough back over itself, to form a long roll, like a Swiss roll, and then bring the ends together, forming a large ring. Put this down in one piece

Filled tortano

Casatiello

on a baking tin and thinly brush the softened lard on the top, bottom and sides of the dough.

Let this rise for 2 hours in a warm place, then bake it in a 190 C/375 F/gas 5 oven for 30 minutes. Serve hot or cold.

182 CASATIELLO

This is a complicated but delicious recipe which, like the Stuffed tortano, comes from traditional Neapolitan cooking. For six people you will need:

400 g/14 oz preferably strong white flour, or plain flour, plus extra for dusting
Pinch of salt   60 g/2½ oz lard plus extra for brushing
25 g/1 oz fresh yeast or 12 g/½ oz dried active baking yeast, dissolved in a little
     lukewarm water   Freshly ground black pepper
100 g/4 oz grated Parmesan cheese   6 small eggs

Blend the flour, a pinch of salt, lard and the dissolved yeast in water together, adding enough water, little by little, and kneading it to get a rather soft dough. Put this dough in a bowl dusted with flour, cover with a towel and let it rise for 1½ hours in a warm, draught-free place. Pull off about 50 g/2 oz of the dough and set it aside. Put the rest on a pastry board and roll it out into a rectangle about 10 mm/⅓ in thick.

Now brush lard thinly over the rectangle, sprinkle with pepper and 10 ml/2 tsp Parmesan and fold it in two. Again, spread lard over the top (which is now half the size of the original rectangle), and sprinkle with 10 ml/2 tsp Parmesan and a little pepper. Fold this one in two, so that you have a piece one-fourth the size of the original rectangle. Then roll it out into a rectangle again, with a thickness of 10 mm/⅓ in as in the beginning. Repeat this whole process twice, sprinkling the rest of the cheese on top. The last time fold it so it forms a long narrow rectangle and do not roll it out again, but form it into a roll with your hands and shape the roll into a circle, pressing the ends together to form a large ring. Put the ring on a greased baking tin and let the dough rise for 3 hours in a warm, draught-free place. Then, make six small evenly-spaced indentations on top, each one half-way into the ring. In each one break a raw egg. Roll out the reserved dough, cut out strips and cover the eggs with them, brushing the edges with water and pressing to seal. Bake in a 150 C / 300 F / gas 4 oven for 20 minutes, then turn the heat up to 200 C / 400 F / gas 6 and bake another 30 minutes, until golden brown.

183   SFOGLIATA

This is another version of the filled ring. For six people you will need:

    400 g / 14 oz preferably strong white flour, or plain flour

    Pinch of salt

    25 g / 1 oz brewer's yeast dissolved in a little lukewarm water

    About 125 ml / 4 fl oz olive oil

Mix the flour with a pinch of salt and the dissolved yeast and add enough of the olive oil, little by little, to obtain a soft smooth dough. Knead it well and then let it rest for 30 minutes in a cool place to rise. Meanwhile prepare the filling. You will need:

500 g / 18 oz onions, the freshest you can find, chopped

45 ml / 3 tbls olive oil   100 g / 4 oz black olives, stoned and chopped

3 anchovy fillets, washed and chopped

200 g / 7 oz tomatoes, blanched, peeled, seeded and chopped

15 ml / 1 tbls capers   12 g / $\frac{1}{2}$ oz finely chopped parsley

75 g / 3 oz Pecorino or Romano cheese, grated

Sauté the onions in the oil over medium-low heat until soft, add the olives, tomatoes, anchovies, capers and the parsley, stir, and let them cook about 5 minutes. Just before you remove it from the oven, add the cheese, stir well and set aside.

Roll out the dough into a rectangular sheet about 10 ml / $\frac{1}{3}$ in thick. It must be this thick or the dough will split when you roll it. Spread some of the filling over one half of the dough, leaving a margin about 25 mm / 1 in wide on all sides. Fold over the other half, spread a little more of the filling over half of it, and roll it again. Continue this way, filling and then rolling the dough over it, until you have formed a big roll. Now shape it into a ring, bringing the ends together. Put it on a greased baking tin, moisten with a little olive oil and bake it at 200 C / 400 F / gas 6 for about 25 minutes. When it is ready, take it out of the oven and let it cool a little before slicing.

Sfogliata

184   FOCACCIA WITH MOZZARELLA [1]

This is an old Neapolitan recipe. For six people you will need:
  6 slices of wholemeal bread, about 10 mm / $\frac{1}{3}$ in thick
  Butter or lard
  800 g / 1$\frac{3}{4}$ lb Mozzarella in slices
  2 medium-sized eggs, beaten
  12 g / $\frac{1}{2}$ oz parsley, chopped, or fresh basil leaves, wiped and chopped
  Freshly ground black pepper

Grease a baking tin, large enough to hold the bread so the slices touch but do not overlap, leaving no empty spaces. Cover these slices with the Mozzarella slices, again leaving no bread uncovered. The cheese can overlap a little. Garnish with the parsley or basil, cover with the beaten eggs and a sprinkling of pepper and bake in a 200 C / 400 F / gas 6 oven for 20 minutes. A nice golden crust forms which is crisp and savoury.

A variation is to add small bits of washed anchovy fillets with the Mozzarella slices.

185   FOCACCIA WITH MOZZARELLA [2]

This is a red version of pizza with Mozzarella, because it uses tomatoes. You will need 6–8 medium-sized tomatoes, blanched, peeled, seeded and cut in wedges, then spread over the Mozzarella. The rest is the same as recipe **184**.

186   FOCACCIA WITH POTATOES

This *focaccia* is a delicious morsel from the Neapolitan kitchen made with a very special dough. For six people you will need:
  400 g / 14 oz plain flour
  100 g / 4 oz potatoes, peeled, boiled and mashed
  20 g / $\frac{3}{4}$ oz fresh yeast or 10 g / $\frac{1}{3}$ oz dried active baking yeast, dissolved in a little lukewarm water

Add a pinch of salt to the flour and then mix it with the potatoes and the dissolved yeast. Add more water, little by little, until you have a rather soft dough. Knead well. Let the dough rest about 1 hour, covered with a cloth in a warm, draught-free place. Roll out six circles, none more than 10 mm / $\frac{1}{3}$ in thick. Put them onto a greased baking sheet, garnish to taste with boiled potatoes, cut into fingers and brushed with olive oil, or with any pizza topping and bake in a 180 C / 350 F / gas 4 oven for 30 minutes.

187   TORTA RUSTICA WITH GREENS

The *torta rustica*, or country quiche, is a rustic tart which only uses one sheet of dough. It is laid out on a baking tin and the filling is spread over it before baking. To make the dough you will need:
  400 g / 14 oz preferably strong white flour, or plain flour
  Pinch of salt
  25 g / 1 oz brewer's yeast, dissolved in a little lukewarm water

Mix the flour, salt and dissolved yeast, adding more water, little by little, until you have a soft but elastic dough. Knead this dough a few minutes, then shape it into a ball and cut a cross into the top. Cover with a cloth and let it rise in a warm, draught-free place for 2 hours. Knead it again and spread it over a greased round 25 cm / 10 in flan tin so it is about 15 mm / $\frac{1}{2}$ in thick and large enough to extend up the sides a little. You can spread over 1.4 kg / 3 lb whatever trimmed, boiled, drained and chopped greens are in season on it, mixed with a little soft cheese such as Ricotta

Focaccia with potatoes

and a pinch of salt and pepper. Moisten the pie with a little oil and put it in a 180 C / 350 F / gas 4 oven for about 45 minutes.

A variation of this is to let the prepared greens brown first in 30–45 ml / 2–3 tbls olive oil, along with a little salt and pepper and a few pieces of chopped anchovy fillets. Or you can sauté a little finely chopped onion in olive oil with chopped anchovy fillets and add the boiled and chopped greens to them before spreading this over the dough.

188   TORTA RUSTICA WITH ONIONS AND TOMATOES

This version calls for lots of onions. You will need about 800 g/1¾ lb of thinly sliced onions which are sautéed in a little olive oil. Add salt, pepper, chopped parsley, thyme, and mint if wished. Off the heat you add 2 beaten eggs, 100 ml/4 fl oz single cream and enough bread crumbs to make a soft but not fluid mixture. Blanch, peel, seed and slice 800 g/1¾ lb tomatoes and set them aside. Roll out the dough and line a large flan tin with the dough as in recipe **187** and over it spread the onions, then the tomatoes, moisten with a little olive oil and bake.

189   TORTA RUSTICA WITH SPINACH

For six people you will need:

Dough recipe **187**   900 g/2 lb spinach or beet spinach
3 medium-sized eggs, beaten   200 g/7 oz Ricotta cheese
75 g/3 oz Parmesan cheese, grated   Freshly grated black pepper
4 anchovy fillets, washed and chopped

Parboil the spinach or greens in a small amount of water, drain very well and chop it finely. Mix the eggs with the spinach, then the cheeses, the anchovy fillets, and a little pepper. Mix well to blend the flavours. Have the dough ready as in recipe **187**. Spread the mixture over it, moisten with oil and bake as in recipe **187**.

190   TORTA RUSTICA WITH RICOTTA AND CHEESE

Prepare the dough as in recipe **187**. For the filling you will need:

300 g/11 oz Ricotta cheese
200 g/7 oz Fontina or Gruyère cheese, cubed
6 medium-sized egg yolks

Torta rustica with onions and tomatoes

Torta rustica with spinach

30–45 ml/2–3 tbls melted butter

Mix the cheeses, egg yolks, salt, pepper and the melted butter together to get a soft but well-blended filling. Use this to fill the *torta rustica*, following the instructions in recipe **187**.

191 TORTA RUSTICA WITH HAM AND MOZZARELLA

Prepare the dough as in recipe **187**. Make the filling with:

    200 g/7 oz prosciutto or cooked ham, or half prosciutto or ham and salami

    150 g/5 oz Mozzarella or smoked Provolone cheese or a combination of both, diced

    3 medium-sized eggs, beaten

    30–45 ml/2–3 tbls, or more, milk or melted butter

    Oregano

    Salt and freshly ground black pepper

Mix the ham and cheese together. Pour the eggs over the ham and cheese. Season with a pinch of oregano and salt and pepper. Add the milk or butter by the spoonfuls to bind the mixture and get just the right consistency, not too dry and not too moist. Then continue as in recipe **187**.

192 PANDORATO [1]

This is an Italian version of French toast. For six people you will need 6 slices of white bread, about 25 mm/1 in thick. Trim away the crusts and cut the bread into strips 4 cm/1½ in wide and 7.5 cm/3 in long. Put them in a shallow pan and soak them in lukewarm milk, about 50 ml/2 fl oz for each slice, and spreading each with a spoonful of beaten egg – two eggs in all should be enough – and sprinkling with salt. Leave them like this for 1 hour so they absorb as much of the milk and egg as possible. Fry them in plenty of hot olive oil. When they are golden on both sides remove them and drain them well. Sprinkle with salt and pepper and serve hot.

193 PANDORATO [2]

This is the same as the recipe described above except that you make a small hollow in each strip with the tip of a knife and in it you put a little piece of Mozzarella cheese and anchovy fillet. Let it soak in the milk and egg and continue as in recipe **192**.

194 FARINATA [1]

This time chick pea flour enters the picture. This humble but tasty, colourful dish is part of the traditional cooking of Liguria. The most common recipe, for 6, calls for:

500 g / 18 oz chick pea flour

About 1.4 L / 2½ pt water

Pinch of salt

Mix the flour and water together with the salt to get a very fluid batter. This must rest 12 hours, usually overnight. After it has rested, carefully remove the scum which will have formed on the top. Stir what is left.

Now pour 100 ml / 4 fl oz olive oil in a very large baking pan and spread it around well. Pour the *farinata* batter over this and stir it so that the oil is absorbed. Bake in a 230 C / 450 F / gas 8 oven and when the top becomes a rather dark golden yellow it is done. Let it cool a little and serve it cut into pieces, sprinkled with a little pepper, if wished.

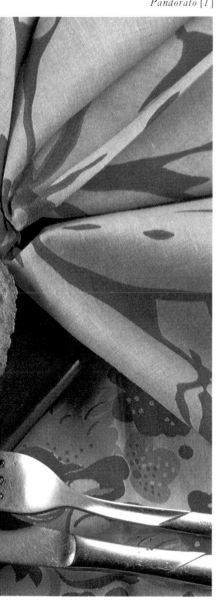

Pandorato [1]

195 FARINATA [2]

In a typical variation of the western Ligurian coast, sprinkle thinly sliced raw onions over the dough before baking.

196 FARINATA[3]

In another variation, the *farinata* is at least 25 mm / 1 in thick and chopped rosemary is spread over it.

197 PANICCIA

This is a Piedmont version of the *farinata*. Warm the water, then off the heat, slowly pour the chick pea flour into it. Stir it well then put it back on the heat, stirring constantly so that it forms a rather solid dough, like polenta. Pour this hot dough onto a pastry board or large plate forming a round about 12 mm / ½ in thick. Spread a little olive oil and some chopped onions on top, add salt and pepper, slice and serve immediately.

198 GRISSINI

Grissini, or bread sticks, are perhaps the thinnest form of bread and can be made at home. They come from the Piedmont region and date back to the 17th century. A kind of light, salty biscuit, they add a touch of elegance to any table. You will need:

400 g / 14 oz preferably strong white flour, or plain flour

Pinch of salt

20 g / ¾ oz brewer's yeast, dissolved in a little tepid water

100 ml / 4 fl oz vegetable oil

Milk

Mix the flour and salt and add the dissolved yeast, the oil and then enough milk, little by little, to make a soft but firm, well-kneaded dough. Let this dough rest for 30 minutes, then knead it again briefly and divide it into pieces. Roll out each piece into long thin strips, to the length and thickness you prefer. Grease a large baking sheet with oil and spread the strips over it. Bake in a 230 C / 450 F / gas 8 oven for 10–15 minutes or until they become crisp and golden.

Sometimes aromatic herbs like rosemary are blended into the dough or even finely chopped onions, garlic or whatever your taste and imagination inspire you to.

199   PANELLE

The *panelle* is a very simple food from Sicily or more exactly, Palermo. Carefully made it is very appetizing. For six people you will need:

600 g / 21 oz chick pea flour
Water
Olive or other vegetable oil

Pour enough water in a pan with the chick pea flour to make a very thick but fluid batter. Bring this to a boil and cook it until you have a creamy mixture. Pour it over a marble slab wiped with oil so that it is about 3 mm / $\frac{1}{8}$ in thick. Let this cool, then cut it into various shapes. Heat a generous amount of hot oil and fry the panelle in this till golden brown. Serve hot.

200   TORTA PASQUALINA

This is a puff-pastry like dough with a spinach and Ricotta filling that has hard-boiled eggs embedded in it. It is called an Easter torte because it is traditionally served at that time of year. In Liguria it is still a central part of the Easter ritual; the vegetables and eggs symbolize the return of life in the spring. It is a dish requiring time and patience and therefore is made less frequently now. Attempts to simplify or modify it have often proved disappointing. But though time-consuming, it is well worth the effort. The original recipe is given below. It serves many people. For the dough you will need:

1 kg / $2\frac{1}{4}$ lb flour
Pinch of salt
60 ml / 4 tbls olive oil

Mix the flour, salt and the olive oil, then knead them with just enough water, added little by little, to make a soft but smooth dough. Divide this dough into 14 equal portions and set them aside on a floured cloth, covered with a dampened cloth. For the filling you will need:

1 kg / $2\frac{1}{4}$ lb spinach, cleaned and stems removed
45 ml / 3 tbls grated Parmesan cheese
600 g / 21 oz Ricotta cheese
Salt
30 ml / 2 tbls plain flour
200 ml / 7 fl oz single cream
12 small eggs
Vegetable oil
Butter, melted
Grated Parmesan cheese, for topping
Vegetable oil

Simmer the spinach about 4 minutes, drain, then squeeze out the excess water and chop it roughly. Mix it in a bowl with the Parmesan and a pinch of salt. Set aside. In another bowl, combine the Ricotta, flour, cream and salt to taste.

Roll out 13 of the 14 portions of dough into rounds to fit inside a loose-bottomed greased 25 cm / 10 in cake tin with sides 5 cm / 2 in high. The last portion of dough should be rolled out so that it is large enough to cover the pan and go up the sides and extend slightly over the rim.

Grease the pan and lay the larger piece of dough inside, letting it extend over the edge. Brush it with vegetable oil, then lay one of the other circles on top. Brush that one with oil and continue layering and brushing the dough, one on top of the other, always brushing each one until you have seven layers.

On top of the seventh layer, spread the spinach mixture. Dribble a little oil over it. Then pour the Ricotta mixture over that. Make 12 small wells in the mixture with

the bottom of a spoon and break a small egg into each one. Put a small amount of melted butter, a pinch of salt and bit of grated Parmesan on top of each egg.

Very gently cover them with another circle of dough and brush a little vegetable oil on top of it. Continue to layer and brush with oil until all the layers have been used. The top layer should be brushed with oil, then the edges of the stack sealed by pressing the first larger layer against the stack, using wet fingers. Prick the top with a fork so the steam can escape during cooking.

Bake in a hot 190 C / 375 F / gas 7 oven for 1 hour. Let cool, remove from the tin and serve either warm or cool, never hot.

Artichokes may be substituted for the spinach. Use only the tenderest leaves and hearts of the artichokes for this.

Torta Pasqualina

These humble yet delicious *schiacciate,* or biscuits, made of chestnut flour, come from Tuscany. Not so long ago the chestnut was an important food source for the poor mountain folk in the Apennines and the Alps. They were served whole, also made flour from them which they made into a kind of bread. It was made as follows. You will need:

> 500 g / 18 oz chestnut flour
>
> A pinch of salt added to cold water

Make a dough with the chestnut flour and salted water, adding it little by little, until you get a rather stiff but moist dough. Form the *schiacciate* into round flat shapes and bake them in the oven on a greased sheet at 200 C / 400 F / gas 6 for about 10 minutes.

Traditionally they are made with a special utensil which has a pair of hinged jaws on a long handle. The dough is put inside the jaws, giving it its traditional round flattened shape, and then it is exposed directly to the fire which should be made from aromatic wood, preferably on the family hearth, for a few minutes. They are traditionally eaten with delicious Ricotta cheese, freshly made in summer. It's true that it is hard to find all these things, the hearth, the implements, the Ricotta, but even cooked on an ordinary baking sheet in an ordinary oven, they are worth the effort.

Necci

Castagnaccio

202   CASTAGNACCIO

The castagnaccio can be considered a sweet, one in fact that was most beloved by children, at least it was several decades ago. It was sold steaming hot on the streets in the autumn, something savoury and friendly when you had to go back to school and the cold was beginning to redden your nose.

The castagnaccio is not just a sweet, otherwise it would not be included in this book. It is more, a complete food, in which the sweetness, very limited in this version, blends with the other ingredients in wonderful harmony. For six people you will need:

    500 g / 18 oz chestnut flour, sifted so it has no lumps
    Pinch of salt in cold water
    Fennel seeds
    Pine nuts
    Raisins, revived in warm water
    Vegetable oil

Mix the chestnut flour in a bowl with the salted water, adding it little by little, using a ladle or whisk to get a semi-liquid but thick batter. Pour this batter in a deep pie dish that you have greased well and on top sprinkle fennel seeds, pine nuts and raisins and moisten the top with oil. Bake in a 200 C / 400 F / gas 6 oven till it is cooked and the top has formed a nice crust. Eat the *castagnaccio* just warm or cold.

Note: The version of *castagnaccio* just described is from Liguria. There is also a Tuscan version which adds olive oil and sugar to the dough and sprinkles rosemary leaves with the pine nuts and raisins on top. It is this Tuscan version which can really be classified as a sweet.

203   FRISEDDE

This is also a toasted bread typical of Puglia which goes well with peasant dishes. For 6 people you will need:

    600 g / 21 oz plain flour
    Pinch of salt
    25 g / 1 oz brewer's yeast dissolved in a little warm water

Mix the flour and salt, then add the dissolved yeast, adding more water, little by little, as necessary to make a bread-like dough. Knead well. Divide this dough into an even number of little balls, then roll each one out into a sausage shape and shape it into a ring with a hole in the middle. Take two rings and put one on top of the other, pressing them together a little so that they stick. Continue with the others. Let them rest like this for 30 minutes, then bake them in a 190 C / 375 F / gas 5 oven. After 15 minutes, take them out and separate them where they were joined – in Puglia this is done with an iron wire – and put them back in the oven to finish baking.

The *frisedde* are served as a cake-like bread. In Puglia they are moistened with a little water to soften them, without making them soggy, then covered with fresh crushed tomatoes, a sprinkling of salt and oregano and a little green virgin olive oil sprinkled all over.

PART THREE

Recipes from around the world

These are also based on a dough or batter. They include pitta bread, chapati, pirotski and pancakes.

204 PITTA

This is another form of bread dough which puffs up when it bakes so that it opens up like a pocket when you cut it horizontally. It is found in many parts of the Mediterranean, including Sicily. It goes by many names, but it seems fairest to use its Middle Eastern name as it is most common there. For six people you will need:

    400 g / 14 oz plain flour
    Pinch of salt
    25 g / 1 oz fresh yeast or 12 g / $\frac{1}{2}$ oz dried active baking yeast, dissolved in a little
      lukewarm water

Mix the flour and salt, then the dissolved yeast, adding more water, little by little, as necessary to get a soft dough. Knead well. This dough should be left to rise $2\frac{1}{2}$–3 hours. Moreover it should be left in a very wide container such as a bread loaf tin, instead of being shaped in a ball and placed in a rounder pan as is usual for pizza and *focaccia*. After the time has passed, pull off pieces of dough and roll them out into a circle about 3 mm / $\frac{1}{3}$ in thick. Put them in the oven at 230 C / 450 F / gas 8 for 8–10 minutes. When they are golden brown, they will be puffed up like little pillows. They can be cut across the top and filled like a sandwich. Called *falafel,* their most common filling is fried balls of boiled chick peas, mixed with other ingredients. You could, however, fill them with Ricotta or another creamy cheese, chopped greens or whatever suits your fancy.

205 CHAPATI

This bread comes from India and the southeast Asian area and it greatly resembles a pizza, suggesting that they had similar origins. For six people you will need:

    500 g / 18 oz flour, preferably whole-wheat
    Pinch of salt
    15 ml / 1 tbls butter, softened
    Melted butter or oil

Mix the flour and salt and work in the butter. Add enough water, little by little, to make a soft smooth dough. Knead it until it is elastic, then shape it into a ball and let it rest in a cool place, covered with a damp cloth, for 1 hour. Then knead it a little again and divide it into small pieces. Roll them out into circles about 3 mm / $\frac{1}{8}$ in thick. Grease a baking sheet with butter or oil, and bake the *chapati* at 220 C / 425 F / gas 7 until they are golden brown on both sides. When the dough is made according to the rules, the circles will tend to puff up, with one side puffed up a little over the other.

Chapati are either used like bread to accompany various foods, or as little plates which soak up the juices of any food put on top. Bread was used in the same way in the West, through the Middle Ages and beyond. There is no tradition of garnishing the *chapati* with different seasonings as we do with our pizza, though it is often served covered with finely chopped onions and other vegetables and eaten.

206 PARATHA

Parathas are very similar to *chapati* and they are equally widespread in India and other places in southeast Asia. Related to the *chapati,* they are a richer, softer bread and are kneaded longer. For six people, you will need:

    500 g / 18 oz plain flour
    Pinch of salt
    30 ml / 2 tbls softened butter
    30–45 ml / 2–3 tbls butter, melted

Chapati

Mix the flour, salt, butter and as much water as necessary to make a smooth firm dough. Knead it until it is somewhat elastic, then let it rest in a cool spot for an hour, covered with a slightly damp cloth. After 1 hour, knead it a little, then divide it into balls of dough. Flatten each one into a circle about 3 mm / $\frac{1}{8}$ in thick and brush each circle with lukewarm melted butter. Fold it in half and brush it with more butter, then fold it into quarters, brushing one more time with the butter. Roll this little bundle out again to form it back into a circle about 3 mm / $\frac{1}{8}$ in thick. Put them on a baking sheet in a 230 C / 450 F / gas 8 oven until golden brown.

207   POORI

Besides the *chapati*, another kind of pancake, called *poori*, is eaten in India. For six people you will need:

400 g / 14 oz plain flour
Pinch of salt
25 g / 1 oz fresh yeast or 12 g / $\frac{1}{2}$ oz dried active baking yeast, dissolved in a little lukewarm water
30 ml / 2 tbls butter
Vegetable oil

Mix the flour, salt, dissolved yeast and butter together, adding more water as necessary to form a soft but firm dough. Knead it until it is smooth and let it rest for 30 minutes under a damp cloth. Knead it again and divide it into smaller balls of dough. Flatten them into circles about 15 cm / 4 in in diameter and 3 m / $\frac{1}{8}$ in thick. Fry them in hot oil, pressing the edges with a spoon, until golden on both sides, turning once. This takes very little time because they puff up almost right away. Drain them well on absorbent paper and serve immediately.

Stuffed poori

208 STUFFED POORI

Make the circles of dough as above, simply a little thicker and about 15 cm/ 4 in in diameter. The filling can be made in many ways, for example, mixing mashed potatoes with chopped onions sautéed in butter with a little grated fresh ginger and aromatic herbs or hot chillies, or you can mix chopped cooked chicken with an egg and single cream. Another idea is to combine chopped boiled greens with sautéed onions, or eggs and cheese. The stuffing is put on half the dough and then the other half is folded over it, pinching the edges together, then fried in plenty of hot oil.

209 LUCHI

This is a kind of Bengali pancake similar to the *poori*. For 6 people you will need:
  400 g/14 oz whole meal or plain flour
  Pinch of salt
  15 ml/1 tbls softened butter
  Vegetable oil
Mix the flour and salt and blend in the butter and enough water, added little by little, to make a soft smooth dough. Knead it a little then divide it into small balls and flatten them on a floured board to form flat circles about 12.5 cm/5 in in diameter. Fry them in hot oil, pressing the edges with the back of a spoon to make them puff and turning them over until they are crisp and golden on both sides. Drain well. They are delicious hot or cold.

210   STUFFED POLISH PANCAKES

For six make a batter with 300 g / 11 oz plain flour and 3 medium-sized eggs, adding up to 225 g / 8 fl oz milk, little by little, with a pinch of salt, to get a soft, rather fluid but still thick mixture. Let it rest for an hour. Then melt butter in a frying-pan and drop the batter in by spoonfuls. Cook, turning once, but do not let these little pancakes brown. Drain and spread them on a cutting board. For the filling:

    300 g / 11 oz minced meat, cooked, or poultry, cooked and finely chopped
    3 medium-sized eggs
    2–3 medium-sized onions, finely chopped
    Salt and freshly ground black pepper

Combine these ingredients, then put a spoonful on each pancake and roll it over the filling. This forms a kind of roll. Pinch the two ends together to close and dip each one in beaten egg and then in dried bread crumbs. Sauté them in a frying-pan in butter until golden on all sides.

Stuffed Polish pancakes

211 AUBERGINE FRITTERS

As with so many curious delicacies, this simple aubergine fritter comes from China. For six people you will need 3–4 aubergines, peeled and cut into pieces. Process the pieces in a blender with a little water, if necessary, then put the eggplant pulp through a food mill or sieve. Set this stiff purée aside. Make a dough with 500 g / 18 oz plain flour and 5 medium-sized eggs. Add to it the following:

2 medium-sized onions, finely chopped   30 ml / 2 tbls soy sauce
The eggplant purée   Salt   2.5 ml / $\frac{1}{2}$ tsp ground ginger
100 ml / 4 fl oz sake or dry Masala

The batter should be well blended. If it is too thick, add a little water. Heat a good amount of oil in a heavy, preferably iron frying-pan, then drop big spoonfuls of the batter into the hot oil, shaping them as you spoon. Cook until brown on both sides, then drain on absorbent paper and serve hot.

Aubergine fritters

212 FISH DUMPLINGS

This recipe comes from the central area of Africa. It serves six and begins with a dough made with:

  400 g / 14 oz plain flour
  Pinch of salt
  12 g / ½ oz fresh yeast or 6 g / ¼ oz dried active baking yeast dissolved in a little
    lukewarm water

Mix the flour, salt and the dissolved yeast together. Add more water, little by little, as necessary, to get a firm but soft dough. Knead well and let it rest for 30 minutes in a cool place, covered with a cloth. Meanwhile prepare the filling:

  400 g / 14 oz skinned, boneless white fish, boiled and finely chopped
  2 medium-sized onions, thinly sliced
  2 garlic cloves, crushed
  1 green pepper, seeded and pounded in a mortar
  50 g / 2 oz fresh white breadcrumbs soaked in milk, then squeezed out
  Salt and freshly ground white pepper

Combine the filling ingredients. When the dough has rested for 30 minutes, roll it out about 3 mm / ⅛ in thick and cut into squares 10–12.5 cm / 4–5 in per side. Divide the filling up among the squares, putting a little on half the square, then fold the other half over it. Pinch the ends together. Fry the dumplings in hot oil.

These dumplings are often served in Africa with a hot sauce made by sautéing a chopped onion in oil till it is translucent, then adding a little tomato pulp and a little finely chopped hot chilli, with salt and pepper to taste.

213 VIETNAMESE PRAWN BALLS

This is a Vietnamese dish. For 6 people you will need 600 g / 21 oz peeled prawns, finely chopped. Add to this 200 g / 7 oz finely chopped bacon fat, and from this mixture, form the balls. They are cooked in either lard or butter over medium-high heat. In the Orient each is held tightly between two sticks of aromatic wood and put directly over a fire of a brazier and basted occasionally with a little melted butter during cooking.

They are often served dipped in a sauce called *nuoc-nam*, made by marinating fish and fish entrails with oil, hot chillies and spices. You can make a very appetizing sauce much more quickly by mixing oil, mashed anchovy fillets and hot chillies.

214 BLINIS [1]

These are the famous Russian pancakes that often accompany caviar and other delicious things. For six people you will need:

  300 g / 11 oz plain flour
  500 ml / 18 fl oz milk
  2 medium-sized eggs
  Pinch of salt

Mix these ingredients together to make a medium thick batter. Drop it by spoonfuls onto a hot griddle or heavy frying-pan greased with a little oil or butter. The pancakes will take shape and cook quickly as they are so thin they do not even need to be turned over. When they have cooked, they are ready to accompany the caviar. Melted butter or sour cream, chopped onion and chopped hard-boiled egg are also often served with them.

Vietnamese Prawn Balls

215   BLINIS [2]

Prepare the *blini* as in recipe **214**. As each blini is ready, spread over it a little filling made with crumbled Ricotta or a similar cheese, mixed with chopped hard-boiled egg, single cream and, if wished, sugar, cinnamon and raisins for a sweet version. When they are filled, either roll them around the filling or fold them over it like big dumplings and sauté them briefly in a little butter.

216   BLINIS [3]

Prepare the *blini* as in recipe **214**. Then spread them in layers in a cake tin greased with butter. Between the blinis alternate a layer of apple slices and a layer of small dots of butter. You can also sprinkle sugar, cinnamon and ground cloves over the layers. Put this *blini* 'torte' in a 190 C / 375 F / gas 5 oven for about 1 hour.

Blinis [2]

217 PANCAKES

For six people make a batter made with the following:

    200 g / 7 oz plain flour
    2 medium-sized eggs
    400 ml / 14 fl oz soured milk or butter milk
    Vegetable oil

   Blend the ingredients together to get a smooth liquid batter. Let it rest for 30 minutes. Heat 15 ml / 1 tbls of oil in a frying-pan. Pour the batter in by spoonfuls to form small pancakes. Cook, turning once, until golden on both sides. Adjust the heat as necessary so they don't burn. Turn them over when small bubbles break on the surface and the batter loses its shiny appearance. Add a little more oil as necessary. Keep warm and serve with butter and preserves or maple or fruit syrups.

Pancakes

218 TORTILLAS

This is the Mexican version of *schiacciata* or *focaccia*, handed down from their ancient Indian civilizations. They are made of a pre-cooked maize flour and served as bread. Today tortillas are also made of wheat flour but they taste differently than the other. To make them traditionally, first you need to wash dried maize, then soak it overnight in cold water with a little slaked lime, then boil it until the skin begins to peel off.

At that point, take it off the heat, drain and let the corn cool. Then, rub off and discard the skins. Rinse the kernals in cold water. This forms a soft dough called *masa*. You can mix in a few spoonsful of water to make it more malleable, then divide it into walnut-sized balls of dough. Flatten them with your hands until you have a flat circle no more than 3 mm/$\frac{1}{8}$ in thick. Fortunately today you can also buy the maize meal called *Masa Harina*, already prepared, in many gourmet stores selling specialist products. Simply mix 225 g/8 oz *Masa Harina* with 400 ml/14 fl oz water. (Regular corn meal is not a good substitute.) Then roll out small circles of dough.

The *tortillas* are cooked very quickly on clay or metal discs, like the Italian *piadine* or *tigelle*, or directly on a medium-hot ungreased griddle, about 1 minute per side, and should be put in a basket covered with a napkin so they do not cool too much before being served. They replace ordinary bread and can go with most foods.

Tortillas

Green enchiladas

219   GREEN ENCHILADAS

These are a celebrated version of *tortillas*. For six people you will need:

    12 thin *tortillas*, recipe **218**
    12 medium-hot chillies
    2 medium-sized eggs
    100 ml / 4 fl oz milk
    Pinch of salt
    Butter or lard
    Chopped onion
    Mild Cheddar cheese, grated

Roast the chillies, turning them over a flame or under a grill, then peel them. Plunge them in boiling water for a second and then pound them into a paste. Mix the eggs with the milk and salt. Dip the *tortilla* in the milk-egg batter, coating both sides, then fry it briefly in a little butter or lard. Drain well and put a little of the mashed chilli on each hot *tortilla*. Wrap it around to form a roll, if wished, put them on a serving plate and lightly sprinkle with the onion and grated cheese. Serve hot.

220   RED ENCHILADAS

Another variation of the Mexican *tortilla*. For six servings you will need:

    12 thin *tortillas*, recipe **218**
    200 g / 7 oz tomatoes
    6 green chillies
    200 g / 7 oz roast pork, finely chopped
    125 g / 4½ oz mild Cheddar cheese, grated, plus extra to garnish
    2 medium-sized eggs
    100 ml / 4 fl oz single cream

Blanch the tomatoes, then peel and seed them. Roast the chillies, turning them over a flame or under a grill, then peel them. Mix and chop them finely. Add the chopped pork and the cheese. Beat the eggs, then lightly beat in the cream. Soak the *tortillas* in the cream-egg mixture, then fry them briefly in butter or melted lard and drain well. On each *tortilla* spread a little of the filling, and, if wished, roll the *tortilla* up to form a large tube. Sprinkle over grated cheese and serve.

221   BRIK WITH EGGS

This dish, common in Morocco, Algeria and Tunisia, comes from the Turkish word *beurrek*. The differences, however, are substantial, beginning with the dough. Proper equipment is necessary and an unusual ability in preparation as well. The dough is called *malsuca*. To make it you will need 100 g / 4 oz hard-grained semolina flour and a pinch of salt.

Work the semolina flour together with the salt and enough water to make a very soft dough. Let it rest under a cloth for an hour. Then work it again, adding more liquid until it becomes semi-liquid. This dough-batter should be cooked by spoonfuls in a very different way from the classic crêpe.

Traditionally it is made on a curious leather tray with a rounded tin bottom that rises gently towards the top and over a small brazier. When you are ready to begin, you take the ball of dough in your hand and let it drop on the heated tray bottom. The moment it touches the tray, the ball of dough is removed so that only a very thin film of dough stays on the metal. The cooked film is then gently taken off and allowed to cool and dry. Continue this way until you have six ready. Now make the filling. You will need for six people:

    2 small onions
    Coarsely chopped parsley
    Salt and freshly ground black pepper
    6 medium-sized eggs
    Olive oil

Parboil the onions, then slice and mix them with the parsley, adding salt and pepper to taste. Divide this up among six bricks and in the centre break an egg. Fold one side over the other carefully, keeping the egg inside and lightly pinch the edges together. Then gently drop it into hot olive oil and fry a very short time until it is golden on both sides. Serve immediately. The egg inside stays soft so you must be careful not to spill it on yourself when you bite into it. (It is an old joke, at the expense of the ignorant, to give someone a brick for the first time with no advance warning and watch the egg spill out on him. Picasso loved to play this trick on the unsuspecting.) The whole process can, of course, be simplified using a more traditional pancake or phyllo dough, and eliminating Picasso's joke, if wished.

Brik with eggs

222   BRIK WITH POTATOES AND EGGS

This is another popular version of the *brik*. For the filling you will need:

300 g / 11 oz potatoes, boiled, peeled and mashed
1 medium-sized onion, chopped
3 hard-boiled eggs, chopped
25 ml / 1½ tbls chopped parsley
30 ml / 2 tbls capers
Salt and freshly ground black pepper
15 ml / 1 tbls grated lemon zest

Mix the ingredients well and divide the filling among the *brik*. Proceed as in the previous recipe **221**.

223   BRIK WITH MEAT

For this filling you will need:

200 g / 7 oz boiled or roasted meat, finely chopped or pounded to a paste
3 medium-sized hard-boiled eggs, crumbled
1 medium-sized onion, chopped
25 ml / 1½ tbls chopped parsley

Mix these ingredients and divide them among the *brik*. Proceed as in recipe **221**.

224   FISH BRIK

For this filling you can use fish, shellfish or even a mixture of both. You also add crumbled hard-boiled eggs, chopped onions, parsley, salt and pepper, and, if necessary, a drop of oil to soften the mixture.

225   BEURREKS

This Turkish word, probably of Arabic origin, suggests a kind of fried pizza with a meat filling. We don't know who first made it, but from the Turkish word comes the name that today is given to similar little pizzas in North America and to the Italian dish *buricchi*, a kind of pizza made by the Jewish community of Ferrara. This suggests that it may have been the Jews from the East who brought this recipe with them, spreading it to the places they settled.

For six people you will need:

300 g / 11 oz plain flour
Pinch of salt
6 medium-sized egg yolks

Make a dough with the flour, a pinch of salt, the egg yolks and as much water as necessary to make a very soft dough. Let the dough rest in a cool spot for an hour, covered with a cloth. Then roll the dough out as thinly as possible with a rolling pin and your hands. Cut ovals from the dough, 12.5 cm / 5 in long and 5 cm / 2 in wide. Rectangles can also be cut.

For the filling you will need:

400 g / 14 oz Ricotta cheese
500 ml / 18 oz single cream
Salt and freshly ground black pepper

Mix these ingredients until well-blended. Then brush each oval with melted butter and place a small lump ot filling at one end. Fold that end of dough over the filling, but just to cover it. Then fold the covered dough over on itself, and continue until you reach the other end of the dough. The final effect should be the filling forms little waves under the dough. Pinch the open edges together, brush the surface with egg yolks, sprinkle with bread crumbs and fry in plenty of hot olive oil.

Brik with potatoes and eggs

Beurreks [1]

226   MEAT PIROTSKI [1]

This dish, characteristic of the Russian and Polish kitchens, can be classified as a type of dumpling. The dough is rolled out and cut into pieces and different fillings are placed on them. Then they are baked. (As dumplings they can also be boiled and seasoned in various ways.) For six people you will need:

250 g / 9 oz plain flour
Pinch of salt
1 medium-sized egg, beaten
Salt
Chilled butter

Make a dough mixing 150 g / 5 oz of the flour, salt, beaten egg and enough water to make a smooth, firm but pliable dough. Knead well. Shape it into a ball and let it rest for 30 minutes covered with a cloth. Meanwhile, knead a stick of chilled butter to soften it and shape it into a ball.

Now, sprinkle the rest of the flour on the pastry board and spread the dough over it, pressing it with the rolling pin so the dough absorbs the dry flour. Then shape the dough into a square about 25 mm / 1 in thick. On top put the ball of butter and crush it a little, then wrap the dough around it. Flatten the dough with the rolling

Beurreks [2]

pin again but do not work it or knead it. Form another square, again 25 g / 1 in thick. Now, let this rest 2–3 minutes, then fold the square over on itself and roll it out with the rolling pin. Form it into a square, let it rest 2–3 minutes, then fold it again and roll it out. Do this at least five times, seven is better. The last time roll the dough out so that it is 6 mm / ¼ in thick. Cut this sheet into 10 cm / 4 in squares and reserve them.

For the filling you will need:

  150 g / 5 oz boiled veal or beef, finely chopped
  100 g / 4 oz bacon fat, finely chopped
  60 g / 2½ oz fresh bread crumbs, soaked in milk, then squeezed out
  1 medium-sized onion, chopped
  2 medium-sized eggs
  25 ml / 1 tbls fennel seeds or chopped dill
  Salt and freshly ground black pepper
  Egg yolk for brushing

Combine all these ingredients and put a little filling on one half of each *pirotski*. Fold the other side over it to form a triangle and pinch the edges together gently. Brush the surface with egg yolk and put them on a greased baking sheet. Bake at 230 C / 450 F / gas 8 until golden brown, about 15 minutes.

227 MEAT PIROTSKI [2]

Basic *pirotski* dough, recipe **226**. For this filling you will need:

 1 large onion, chopped

 15 ml / 1 tbls butter

 225 g / 7 oz boiled beef, veal or chicken, finely chopped

 6 canned sardines, drained and finely chopped

Sauté the onion in the butter, then mix in the meat and the fish off the heat. Continue as in recipe **226**.

You can make another version of this filling using washed anchovy fillets instead of sardines, along with fresh breadcrumbs soaked in a little milk and squeezed out, and an egg.

You can also make the *pirotski* in the shape of half moons or even rectangles, putting one square over the other and sealing the edges. You can also roll the rectangles of dough around tin tubes and fry them like that, forming hollow rolls, and then stuff them with a filling that does not require further cooking.

Meat pirotski [1]

228   PIROTSKI WITH BRAINS

For six people you will need:

    Basic *pirotski* dough, recipe **226**, formed in hollow tubes and fried

    300 g / 11 oz lambs' brains   45 ml / 3 tbls vinegar

    Salt and black pepper corns   Bay leaf

    1 large onion, chopped   15 ml / 1 tbls butter

    30 ml / 2 tbls plain flour

    30 ml / 2 tbls single cream

    Pinch of freshly grated nutmeg

    25 g / 1 oz chopped parsley

    15 ml / 1 tbls lemon juice

Simmer the brains in water with the vinegar, salt, peppercorns and bay leaf. Drain well and cool. Clean the brains and cut it into pieces.

Sauté the onion in the butter, then add the flour and mix well. Add the cream and stir well, letting it come to a boil. At this point add the brains, then one at a time, the nutmeg, the parsley, salt and just at the last, the lemon juice. Cook the mixture long enough to make a thick sauce which can be used as a filling for the tubes. The tubes should be filled while the fried dough is still warm.

229   PIROTSKI WITH FISH

For six people you will need:

    Basic *pirotski* dough, recipe **226**

    400 g / 14 oz pike or other fresh water fish, boiled, skinned and boned

    45 ml / 3 tbls butter

    1 medium-sized onion, chopped

    1–2 hard-boiled eggs, cubed

    Salt and freshly ground black pepper

Sauté the onion in the butter, then add the fish, the eggs, salt and pepper. Let it cook for a minute to blend then stuff the *pirotski* with this and bake.

230   PIROTSKI WITH LIVER [1]

For six people you will need:

    Basic *pirotski* dough, recipe **226**

    500 g / 18 oz calf's liver, cooked and chopped

    30 ml / 2 tbls butter

    1 large onion, chopped

    2 medium-sized eggs, beaten   Salt and freshly ground black pepper

Brown the onion in the butter, then put it in a bowl. Mix in the liver, eggs, onion, salt and pepper, fill the *pirotski* and bake.

231   PIROTSKI WITH LIVER [2]

For six people you will need:

    Basic *pirotski* dough, recipe **226**

    500 g / 18 oz calf's liver

    50 g / 2 oz chopped bacon fat

    1 medium-sized onion, chopped

    Salt and freshly ground black pepper   2 bay leaves

    15 ml / 1 tbls oil   15 ml / 1 tbls butter

    50 g / 2½ oz fresh white bread crumbs, soaked in milk and squeezed dry

    45 ml / 3 tbls dry Madeira or dry Marsala   15 ml / 1 tbls rum

    Pinch of freshly grated nutmeg

Pirotski with brains

Clean the liver and cut it into thin slices. Sauté the onion in the bacon fat, then add the liver, a little salt and pepper and the bay leaves. Cook very briefly so the liver doesn't get tough. Remove it from the fire and pound it in a mortar, adding little by little, the oil, butter, breadcrumbs, Madeira or Marsala, rum and a pinch of nutmeg and salt. This can also be done in a blender, though the texture is slightly different. In both cases remove the bay leaves from the mixture before beginning. Use this to stuff the triangles and bake as in recipe **226**.

Pirotski with liver [2]

232 PIROTSKI WITH PRAWNS

For six people you will need:
    Basic *pirotski* dough, recipe **226**
    24 medium-sized prawns, boiled, peeled and finely chopped; reserve the shells
    50 g / 2 oz butter   15 ml / 1 tbls flour   30 ml / 2 tbls single cream
    Pinch of freshly grated nutmeg
    Salt and freshly ground black pepper
    3 medium-sized egg yolks, beaten

Pound the shells very well, then sauté them gently in the butter a few minutes and strain it through a fine sieve to make a shrimp butter. Heat the shrimp butter in a small frying-pan, add the chopped prawns, the flour, cream, nutmeg, salt and pepper, stirring constantly. Remove from the heat when the mixture has thickened and add the egg yolks. Stir this over very low heat, watching the mixture carefully so the eggs do not curdle. As soon as it thickens, remove it and fill the *pirotski* and bake.

Pirotski with prawns

Chinese fried bread

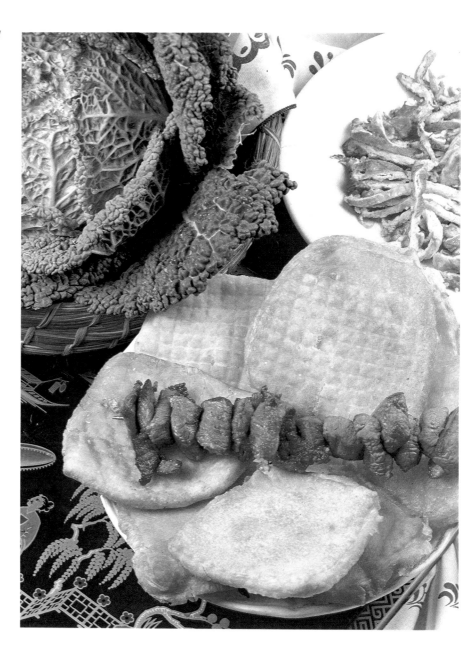

233   CHINESE FRIED BREAD

These are served, like baked bread, with various foods. For six people you will need:

500 g / 18 oz plain flour
Pinch of salt

Work together the flour, salt and enough hot water, added little by little, to make a very firm but pliable dough. Roll it out into a rectangle 20 mm / $\frac{3}{4}$ in thick and cut it into 6 cm / $2\frac{1}{4}$ in squares. Brush half of them generously with oil, and cover with the others. Fry them in pairs in more hot oil.

They can be served, while still hot, with pieces of roasted or boiled meat, an omelette cut into strips, fried bean sprouts moistened with soy sauce, strips of cabbage, browned in a pan and flavoured with soy sauce, and so on.

Quiche Lorraine

234   QUICHE LORRAINE

This celebrated dish is similar to a cheese crostata. For six people you will need:

    200 g / 7 oz flour

    75 g / 3 oz butter, softened   Pinch of salt

Work the flour with the butter and add the salt and enough water to get a soft but firm dough. Roll out a circle about 6 mm / $\frac{1}{4}$ in thick and line a lightly greased quiche tin with it, so that it extends up the sides. Prick the dough with a fork and partially cook it in a hot oven at 200 C / 400 F / gas 6 until the pastry is set but not browned. For the filling you will need:

    250 g / 9 oz smoked bacon or ham   3 medium-sized eggs, beaten

    225 g / 8 oz single cream

    Pinch each of salt and freshly ground black pepper   Butter

Cut the bacon or ham into small pieces and spread them over the pastry. Beat the eggs and add the cream, salt and pepper and pour over the bacon. Put small pieces of butter over the top and bake at 190 C/375 F/gas 5 until the eggs have set and the crust is golden.

235 MEAT KULEBIAKA

This is a kind of *torta rustica* filled with meat and other ingredients from the grand cuisine of Imperial Russia. For six people you will need:

400 g/14 oz plain flour
Pinch of salt
2 medium-sized eggs
150 g/5 oz butter, softened

Add the salt to the flour and work them together with the eggs and butter, adding just enough water to make a very soft but well blended dough. Shape it into a ball and let it rest in a cool place, under a cloth. Meanwhile prepare the filling. You will need:

300 g/11 oz cooked minced meat (left-overs are fine)
2–3 medium-sized onions, chopped and sautéed in butter until soft
200 g/7 oz mushrooms, chopped and sautéed briefly in oil
Salt and freshly ground black pepper
3 medium-sized hard-boiled eggs, cut in wedges
Beaten egg yolk

Blend the meat, onions and mushrooms well with salt and pepper to taste. Roll the dough out into a 6 mm/$\frac{1}{4}$ in thick rectangle and spread the filling over the dough, leaving only a border of about 12 mm/$\frac{1}{2}$ in. On top of the filling place the wedges of hard-boiled eggs pushing them in to the filling a little. Finally roll the dough up over the filling, forming a kind of strudel. Pinch the ends so that the edges stick together and brush the surface with beaten egg yolk. Place it on a well-greased baking pan and put in a 190 C/375 F/gas 5 oven for 25 minutes or until the dough has turned golden brown.

236 FISH KULEBIAKA

This recipe is almost the same as the one above except that you use fish instead of meat with the mushrooms. The onions and hard-boiled eggs are usually omitted. Instead you can substitute parsley and grated lemon zest.

237 CHEESE KULEBIAKA

This kulebiaka is made with a fresh cheese like Ricotta to which you can add eggs, mushrooms, onions, and other vegetables in combination to satisfy almost any taste.

238 MUSHROOM KULEBIAKA

This is almost the same as the cheese kulebiaka except that the main ingredient is 300 g/11 oz mushrooms, while you reduce the cheese to 100 g/4 oz or less. You can also add boiled and cubed potatoes. Two raw, beaten eggs instead of hard-boiled ones can also be incorporated into the filling.

Fish kulebiaka

Index

FOR NOTES AND YOUR OWN RECIPES

FOR NOTES AND YOUR OWN RECIPES

FOR NOTES AND YOUR OWN RECIPES

FOR NOTES AND YOUR OWN RECIPES

FOR NOTES AND YOUR OWN RECIPES

FOR NOTES AND YOUR OWN RECIPES

FOR NOTES AND YOUR OWN RECIPES

FOR NOTES AND YOUR OWN RECIPES